# Small and Medium Sized Enterprises

Compiled by
Kenneth Dyson

Published by Routledge
in association with the University of Bradford and Spicers Centre
for Europe Ltd

First published 1990
by Routledge in association with the University of Bradford and
Spicers Centre for Europe Ltd

Routledge
11 New Fetter Lane, London EC4P 4EE

Transferred to Digital Printing 2004

Simultaneously published in the USA and Canada
by Routledge
a division of Routledge, Chapman and Hall, Inc.
29 West 35th Street, New York 10001

*A catalogue record for this book
is available from the British Library.*

ISBN 0-415-38294

*Library of Congress Cataloging in Publication Data
is also available*

ISBN 0-415-38294

# Small and Medium Sized Enterprises

# SPICERS EUROPEAN POLICY REPORTS

*European Internal Market Policy*
Kevin Featherstone

*The Food Sector*
Stephen Fallows

*Transport Policy*
Kerry Hamilton

*Youth Policy*
Gordon Blakely

*Employment Policy*
Margareta Holmstedt

*Regional Policy*
Colin Mellors/Nigel Copperthwaite

# CONTENTS

# FOREWORD

This volume is one of a series offering an informed guide to particular policies and programmes of the European Community. They are intended for the intelligent reader as well as for the specialist. They assume no prior knowledge of the European Community, but they each offer a comprehensive and up-to-date guide to what the Community is doing, or proposes to do, in important areas of economic, social and political life. The volumes should appeal especially to those involved in business and commerce, public administration, and education.

The volumes guide the reader through the maze of European Community legislation and policy proposals. Their main concern is with the official documents of the European Community institutions: helping the reader to understand Community policies and proposals. By doing so, each volume offers the reader a single reference source, collating all the essential information the reader needs to understand what is going on.

Each volume is structured so as to offer easy access to the specific information needed. A preliminary note explains what the European Community is and how it operates. Each volume focuses on a distinctive policy area, and **SECTION I** introduces the reader to European Community action in that sphere. It explains how Community policy has evolved, the problems currently being confronted, and what is proposed for the future. **SECTION II** highlights the key documents and proposals in the policy area, giving extensive summaries of each of them. Finally, **SECTION III** provides a comprehensive listing of all the relevant Community documents in this policy sphere, with full bibliographical details and a brief note as to their content.

As the reader progresses through each volume, he or

she will have been guided from the general to the very specific, and from little or no knowledge to an informed picture of developments in the policy sphere concerned. Moreover, the information has been structured so as to allow the more specialist reader to pursue particular inquiries yet further: the volumes guide the reader to the policy documents specific to his/her interest.

With the drive to complete the single internal European Community market by the end of 1992, more and more attention will be focused on Community policies and actions. By the end of this century, the European Community will be playing a more prominent part in the lives of its citizens and in a way which will have ramifications in other parts of the world also. The European Community is already an important actor on the world stage, and it will be even less possible to ignore it in the 1990s. This series of policy guides is designed to provide the information that is and will be needed to respond to this changing world. High-quality information is the key to effective action.

This series has been produced by the <u>European Briefing Unit</u> at the <u>University of Bradford (UK)</u> together with <u>Spicers Centre for Europe Limited</u>, a member of Spicer and Oppenheim International. The collaboration between these two bodies has brought together a team of specialist writers expert in the various policy spheres covered by the volumes. Each writer is actively engaged in the study and research of these policy areas, and each has long experience in communicating their skills to the lay audience. The series has been co-ordinated by Amanda Deaville (Spicers) and Kevin Featherstone (Bradford).

Both the European Briefing Unit (EBU) at the University of Bradford and Spicers Centre for Europe have an active interest in promoting knowledge and awareness of the European Community. The EBU is located in the Department of European Studies at the University of Bradford: the Department is the largest of its kind in the UK, and is actively involved in both teaching and research at all levels. The EBU was created in 1988 as a public resource, operating on a non-profit and open access basis. It acts as a neutral forum for the purpose of disseminating and advancing relevant knowledge about the Single European Market; new trading and business opportunities in Europe; the European Community's Structural Funds and technology programmes; the external trade, business and political relations of the EC; and the social, cultural and educational implications of European integration. The EBU exists to serve the needs of industry, commerce and public authorities as well as those of the University itself and other educational bodies. The EBU has established close collaborative links with a number of relevant bodies across different sectors so as to promote its activities.

Spicers Centre for Europe Ltd is a privately based organization serving the needs of its commercial clients. It offers expert EC advice and information to both private and public sector organizations and enterprises. It assists its clients in obtaining funding from EC sources, and it keeps them informed as to the changes in EC policy which might affect their interests. It advises organizations on how they might respond to the opportunities and challenges of the EC, by reviewing corporate strategies. It also offers a business information service based on its own and EC data bases, involving the Tenders Electronic Daily data base (TED) and the Business Co-operation Network data base (BC-NET). As a member of Spicer and Oppenheim International it is linked to an organization which has 250 offices in more than fifty countries throughout the world.

The collaboration between the EBU and Spicers is intended to produce a continuing series of publications to inform both specialist and lay audiences about the role and impact of the European Community. Readers of these volumes are invited to contact either body directly if they have any comments to make on the volumes, or if they would like to know more about the activities of either organization.

Both the EBU and Spicers would like to record their gratitude to Alan Jarvis (Routledge) for his support and patience in dealing with this publishing venture. Moreover, progress would have been more difficult had it

Small and Medium Sized Enterprises

not been for the efficient typing, by Christine Pratt of Spicers.  More generally, thanks go to the full team of writers and assistants involved in this project for their willingness to see it succeed.


Kevin Featherstone
General Editor

Small and Medium Sized Enterprises

Contact addresses:

The European Briefing Unit
University of Bradford
Bradford    BD7 1DP
United Kingdom

Telephone:  0274-733466
Telex:   51309 UNIBFD G
Fax Number:   0274 305340


Spicers Centre for Europe Limited
Ground Floor
10-12 East Parade
Leeds    LS1 2AJ
United Kingdom

Telephone:  0532 442629
Telex:   557890 EUROPE G
Fax Number:   0532 449909

# THE EUROPEAN COMMUNITY: ITS ROLE, INSTITUTIONS, AND LEGISLATION

The European Community (EC) represents a unique development in the world: a new structure of relations between states. It has often been referred to as 'the Common Market' because it is a single trading entity: goods moving between the member countries are not subject to tariffs, while imports from the rest of the world enter under uniform conditions. But it is much more than that: it plays an important political and social role, in addition to its economic purposes. Moreover, the EC is set to develop much further in the 1990s.

In the 1958 Treaty of Rome, a commitment was made to seeking in the long-term 'an ever closer union among the peoples of Europe', an ambitious objective which it has found difficult to realise. However, the Single European Act which came into force in July 1987 provides for an expansion of the EC's political role and for the completion by the end of 1992 of a fully integrated, barrier-free internal market.

The 'European Community' actually stems from three Communities: the European Coal and Steel Community (ECSC) established in 1952; the European Economic Community (EEC) which came into being in 1958; and, the European Atomic Energy Community (Euratom) which also began in 1958.

The original member states of each of these three Communities were Belgium, France, the Federal Republic of Germany, Italy, Luxembourg and the Netherlands. Successive enlargements of the Communities have increased their membership from six to twelve: Denmark, Ireland and the United Kingdom joined as of 1 January 1973; Greece on 1 January 1981; and Portugal and Spain on 1 January 1986. The population of the EC is now 320 million, greater than that of the USA (234 million), the Soviet Union (269 million), or Japan (119 million). Its

Gross Domestic Product per head is significantly lower than that of either the USA or Japan. However, the Community today is the world's largest trading power, accounting for almost 20% of world trade. Economically and politically, the EC dominates Western Europe, and it has established important relations with countries across the world.

Policy making in the EC involves the Commission, the Council of Ministers, the European Parliament, and the Economic and Social Committee, with the adjudication of the Court of Justice and the Court of Auditors. In addition, the European Investment Bank (EIB) was established by the Treaty of Rome as the bank for financing capital investment promoting the balanced development of the Community.

Until 1967, the three original Communities had separate Councils of Ministers and executive Commissions (known as the 'High Authority' in the ECSC). By contrast, the European Parliament and the Court of Justice have been common to the ECSC, EEC and Euratom since 1958. From 1967 onwards there has been a single Commission and a single Council, simplifying the overall structure.

The three most important policy-making institutions of the EC today are the Council of Ministers, the Commission and the European Parliament. Since 1974, they have been joined by the 'European Council', a body given formal status by the Single European Act. The European Council is the term given to the summit meetings of the heads of government (and of state in the case of France) of the EC countries. It has no legislative power, rather its purpose is to place current issues in a more general perspective and to give impetus to those initiatives that it regards as priorities for action. Until 1985, it met three times a year, but this has since been cut back to twice a year. The Presidency of the European Council and of the Council of Ministers rotates between the member governments at six-monthly intervals. The European Council meetings are usually held in the country holding the presidency.

The Council of Ministers' headquarters is in

## Small and Medium Sized Enterprises

Brussels, where the Commission is also based. The European Parliament, by contrast, currently holds its plenary sessions in Strasbourg, most of its committee meetings in Brussels, whilst its permanent staff are based in Luxembourg. This rather awkward compromise remains a source of controversy.

EC legislation is determined by the three main institutions - the Council of Ministers, the Commission, and the European Parliament - with the Economic and Social Committee offering its advisory opinion. The Commission acts as the initiator of legislation and as the executive authority responsible for implementing it. Legislation is finally enacted after it has been approved by the Council of Ministers, either acting unanimously or by a qualified majority. It has been estimated that, as a result of the Single European Act, two-thirds of the internal market proposals will be covered by majority voting. The Council's legislative role has been further amended by a new 'Co-operation Procedure' established by the Single European Act, which gives increased powers to the European Parliament. This provides, _inter alia_, for the Parliament to be able to reject the Council's initial response to a Commission proposal, and the Council can then only pass the proposal into law if it acts unanimously (Art. 149: 2c of the EEC Treaty as amended). Prior to the Single European Act, the Parliament already had the final say over the annual EC budget, though its scope for manoeuvre on expenditure is set within limits.

Some description of each institution is necessary. The Council of Ministers is made up of representatives of the governments of the twelve Member States. Each government normally sends one of its ministers. Its membership thus varies with the subjects down for discussion. The Foreign Minister is regarded as his country's 'main' representative in the Council, but Ministers for Agriculture, Transport, Economic and Financial Affairs, Social Affairs, Industry, the Environment and so on also meet frequently for specialized Council meetings and sometimes sit alongside the Foreign Ministers. The Council is supported by a large number of working parties and by a Committee of

8

Permanent Representatives (COREPER). COREPER is composed of the various national 'ambassadors' to the EC.

The Commission consists of seventeen members, appointed by agreement between the member governments. Throughout their four-year term of office, Commissioners are required to remain independent of national governments. An individual Commissioner cannot be sacked: the Parliament can pass a motion of censure compelling the Commission to resign en bloc.

The European Parliament is the world's first directly elected international assembly. It was first directly elected in 1979: it was previously composed of nominated national parliamentarians. The Parliament serves five-year terms and currently has 518 members (MEPs).

The Court of Justice, based in Luxembourg, acts as the supreme court of the EC. It should not be confused with the European Court of Human Rights in Strasbourg, which is not an EC body. The Court of Auditors began operating in 1977 and, as its name suggests, it audits the EC accounts. The Economic and Social Committee is an advisory body of 189 members, representing various sectors of economic and social life, offering opinions on EC policies and proposals.


## EC Law

The nomenclature of EC legislation can be confusing. The essential point to bear in mind is that the Commission brings forward proposals for legislation, the outcome of which will be variously determined by the Council and the Parliament. 'Primary legislation' of the EC is embodied in the treaties; 'Secondary legislation' is derived from the treaties in the form of 'Regulations', 'Directives' etc. The EC represents a distinct legal system, and its strongest form of legislation is superior to national law.

When acting under the Treaty of Paris (ECSC), the Commission can take decisions, make recommendations or issue opinions. Decisions are binding in their entirety; recommendations are binding as to the ends but not as to the means; opinions are not binding. The Council acts in ECSC affairs mainly at the request of the Commission, either stating its opinion on particular issues or giving the assent without which, in certain matters, the Commission cannot proceed. The Commission's ECSC decisions are mostly addressed to individual persons, firms or governments but they may also lay down general rules, since the Commission does also have general rulemaking powers.

When acting under the Rome Treaties (EEC and Euratom), the Council and the Commission issue regulations, directives, decisions, recommendations and opinions. Regulations are of general application: they are binding in their entirety and applicable in all member states. Directives are binding on the member states to which they are addressed as regards the results to be achieved, but leave the form and methods of achieving it to the discretion of the national authorities. Decisions may be addressed to a government, an enterprise or a private individual; they are binding in their entirety on those to whom they are addressed. Recommendations and opinions are not binding.

The discrepancy in terminology between the Paris Treaty and the two Rome Treaties is confusing. An ECSC 'recommendation' is a binding enactment corresponding to the EEC and Euratom 'directive', whereas an EEC 'recommendation' is not binding and is not stronger than an 'opinion'. When examining the current progress of EC legislation in non-ECSC policy areas, the reader typically focuses on Commission proposals (e.g. for a directive) to be agreed by the Council of Ministers (subject to the differential powers of the European Parliament).

It is clear from the above that the EC today is an important actor in international relations, enjoying both political and economic significance not only for its domestic citizens but also for those in other countries.

## PREFACE

Readers of the volume should note at the outset that in the EC 95% of enterprises are SMEs and that they contribute some 50% of total industrial employment which varies in member states from 43% to 75%. The European Commission has identified a major role for SMEs in developing the innovative and exporting capacity of the EC, either directly or indirectly through subcontracting with larger enterprises. At the same time SMEs face particular difficulties related to their size. Accordingly, the EC has an important role to play in reducing the burdens on SMEs and in assisting them through advice and support structures.

The author would like to express his particular thanks to the staff of DG XXIII for their assistance in the preparation of this volume and to Denis Healey of the Office of the UK Permanent Representative in Brussels for his encouragement and support. Neither he nor the staff of DG XXIII are in any way responsible for any factual errors or mistakes of interpretation. I am also most grateful to Grace Hudson, European Documentation Centre librarian at the University of Bradford, for all her efforts in helping to chase references.

Kenneth Dyson

**SECTION I**
**INTRODUCTION**

# THE EUROPEAN COMMUNITY AND THE DEVELOPMENT OF SME POLICY

Since 1986, till the end of the first Delors
Commission at the end of 1988, no EC policy field -
other than the internal market programme itself - can
claim to have been as high profile as SME policy. At
the outset it is necessary to establish how and why this
priority arose - in other words, the chronology and the
origins and rationale of SME policy. The political
priority given to this policy became most apparent in
1986: in January, following the accession of Spain and
Portugal to the Community, the European Commission
conferred on one of its new Spanish members, Abel
Matutes, specific responsibility for SMEs; in June an
independent SME Task Force (with a staff of
approximately forty) was established in the Commission;
and on 3 November the Action Programme for Small and
Medium Sized Enterprises was unanimously adopted by the
Council. Matutes' concept of a 'Europe of enterprise'
was underlined in the Council Resolution of 30 June 1988
on 'the improvement of the business environment and
action to promote the development of enterprises,
especially Small and Medium Sized Enterprises in the
Community'. The first point to note is that, during
this period, SME policy underwent a learning process
during which the concept of enterprise subsumed that of
SMEs and cross-national networking emerged as the major
theme of the EC's policy.

Secondly, it is important to emphasize that SME
policy represented a broad horizontal function within
the European Commission. A SME dimension exists in
virtually every EC policy area: for instance, DG V was
involved through local employment initiatives,
management training for SMEs, COMETT and EUROTECNET as
well as through health and safety measures; DG XVI
through the European Business and Innovation Centres and
the growing importance of European Regional Development

15

Small and Medium Sized Enterprises

Fund (ERDF) measures to promote 'indigenous development potential' of areas; DG XV through taxation and company law issues; DG VI through rural development issues; DG II through the New Community Instrument (NCI); and DG XIII through innovation and technology transfer issues (notably the SPRINT programme). In other words, SME policy was caught up in a complex field of bureaucratic and political forces. The ambition for an integrated and coherent policy towards SMEs lived in permanent tension with the real fragmentation of policies. These enormous difficulties of co-ordination reflected the sheer complexity of SME problems, and the multiplicity of tools evolved to meet them, as well as the structural complexity and administrative politics within the Commission itself. The second interest of SME policy lies in the fact that, despite these difficulties, the SME Task Force presided over a process of cultural change within the Commission, towards the values of 'enterprise culture'.

Thirdly, the definition of the object of the EC's SME policy remained contentious. The SME Task Force noted that in practice the definition of SMEs varied from country to country and from sector to sector. It chose to adopt the definition used by the European Investment Bank (EIB) and by the European Structural Funds. A SME is an independent enterprise with less than 500 employees whose fixed assets (net of depreciation) are less than 75 million ECUs (European Currency Units) and in whose capital structure a large enterprise holds no more than a one-third participation. Various difficulties are raised by the sheer breadth of this definition. If the maximum workforce is fixed at 500, SMEs account for more than 95% of companies within the Community and provide more than two-thirds of total employment (approximately 60% in industry and over 75% in services). In terms of legal structure and type of activity the range is enormous: from one-person companies to co-operatives, from 'high-tech' new starts to traditional workshops, from independent operators to sub-contractors. The definition also suffers from the weakness that, other than the criterion relating to capital held by a larger firm, no account is taken of

the relationships between firms. There is the further
dilemma between preferences for the very smallest
companies (e.g. with regard to company account
requirements) and encouragement of growth. By applying
special conditions related to size one may perversely be
encouraging companies to stay below a certain size in
order to retain exemptions.

In practice, the EC's SME policy became entrapped in
a tension between a 'clientelist' orientation and a
'functional' orientation. Was it there to serve a
particular client group, defined in terms of enterprise
size? Or was the function of the EC's SME policy to
promote enterprise? In the latter case one could not
realistically assume that all the client group would be
responsive to the enterprise challenge. From an
enterprise perspective it was clear that SME policy
embraced very different enterprises indeed. Inexorably,
the issue arose of whether the size of an enterprise was
decisive. For the large majority of small businesses
the aim of independence might be more highly prized than
growth and job creation; direct support schemes for SMEs
might carry too unacceptable a 'cost' in terms of
outsider interest and influence. It seemed far more
important that an enterprise is specialized in a
particular product or small set of products of high
quality and in a niche market; and that its management
has the personal qualities of tenacity, stamina and the
ability to work long hours. De facto, under the
umbrella of an enterprise policy for the Community, SME
policy began to refine its position towards a less over
optimistic view of the capabilities of the small
business sector. It remained desirable to promote local
artisans and very small companies; after all, in areas
of the EC affected by rapid decline of employment in
manufacturing industry and in agriculture, there was
often no practical alternative. At the same time SME
policy had to confront the reality that local artisans
and very small companies were least likely to be
interested in developing within European markets and
were, therefore, least likely to be interested in the
mechanisms developed by the SME Task Force and by DG
XIII. Medium-sized companies, and a small subset of

'upwardly mobile' small companies, were <u>de facto</u> the increasingly important targets of SME policy. They were more likely to have the internal capacity to develop within Europe. When, in January 1989, the SME Task Force was redeployed to form the major element in the new DG XXIII, SME policy did not disappear. It was, however, more clearly translated into 'enterprise policy' in the title of the new directorate general.

## The Rationale of EC Policy for SMEs

The rise to political prominence of SME policy within the European Community during the 1980s is a complex story. It involves internal factors within the European Commission, in particular perceptions of the failure of specific social, regional and industrial policies; external factors, notably the United States' model of job generation through small businesses in contrast to unemployment levels within the EC persistently higher than the OECD average; and the challenge of radical restructuring of the business structure with the completion of the Single European Market, a programme that was driven by pressure from large companies like Philips and that raised the issue of 'who is to benefit?' in a newly dramatic form.

From the late 1970s onwards the inadequacy of the EC's industrial, regional and social policies was thrown into sharper relief. Unemployment mounted, not least with the rapid decline of jobs in the traditional manufacturing industries (e.g. steel, shipbuilding, textiles); EC policy actually contributed to this process e.g. the coal and steel restructuring measures; whilst regional and local disparities of economic performance mounted. The ERDF (DG XVI) began, from 1980, to shift away from reliance just on measures to bolster public investment in the infrastructure of regions whose development was lagging. New measures to exploit 'the indigenous development potential' were launched under the 'non-quota' section of the ERDF Regulation in 1980 (specific Community measures for steel, shipbuilding, textile and clothing, and fishery areas); expanded under the 1984 Regulation, in particular the Community programmes - notably STAR and VALOREN, for advanced telecommunications and energy exploitation respectively, and RENAVAL and RESIDER, conversion of shipbuilding and steel areas - and national programmes of Community interest (NPCIs); and further strengthened in the Council Regulation of 19 December 1988, notably the new mechanism of 'global grants' to help SMEs.

Also, particularly from 1983, DG V (Employment, Social Affairs and Education) began to recognize the role of local employment initiatives (LEIs) as a source of employment creation and the need to develop support activities for local development agencies. Commission Communication of November 1983 on Community Action to Combat Unemployment - Contribution of Local Employment Initiatives was followed by the Council Regulation of June 1984 Concerning the Contribution of LEIs to Combating Unemployment. In addition to more aid for separate specific projects from the European Social Fund (ESF), DG V established ELISE (the European Information Exchange Network on Local Employment Initiatives), and launched a new action programme on economic development and local employment in 1986 along with an exchange programme between local development agents in the member states.

Another indicator of the growing perception of the importance of SMEs within the Commission was the development of the New Community Instrument. NCI II, authorized in 1982, specified for the first time SMEs as one of three priorities for financing; NCI III (1983), NCI IV (1986) and the proposed NCI V have reflected an increasing commitment to SMEs. These policy developments represented a learning process in particular policy areas about the inadequacy of existing measures.

Externally, the comparatively better economic performance of the EC's main competitors, the United States and Japan, prompted new questions about the characteristics of their economic structures that promoted success. In its 1985 Report on Improving Community Competitiveness and Industrial Structures the

## Small and Medium Sized Enterprises

European Commission emphasized the role of SMEs as an important source of employment creation, economic innovation and regional regeneration. Emphasis was placed on the key role of small enterprises in the American and Japanese economies: e.g. 'high-tech' new starts and business incubator centres, 'spin-offs' from large enterprises, corporate venturing and sub-contracting arrangements. In short, economic theories of the advantages of large production units exploiting 'economies of scale' were reconsidered. With increasing size enterprises seemed to suffer from the mounting inefficiencies of long and complex management chains, especially the expansion of middle management, and from deteriorating labour relations. Faced also with mounting technological complexity and accelerating market change, large companies began to seek new means of operation. Instead of continuing to do everything in-house, companies like Philips, BMW and Siemens began increasingly to seek to hive off many activities to small outside suppliers - in short, to invest in developing a network of strong suppliers. Sub-contracting of manufacturing and design work involved in turn forging a new type of relationship based on partnership and close contact.

Four developments in particular seemed to point the way to an increasingly important role for SMEs. Firstly, with the shortening of product cycles they had the flexibility of simple management structures to innovate and adapt rapidly. Secondly, new developments in information and communication technologies, notably the introduction of computer-aided design and manufacturing, gave SMEs increasingly powerful control systems and enabled a greater variety of products to be designed and produced more cheaply. Thirdly, their role as innovators and sources of dynamism was being revealed in the computer industry and was expected to underpin the next phase of economic growth. Fourthly, the great growth in output and employment in the service sector that many countries, notably the United States, had experienced had taken place predominantly in small enterprises. Within the labour market, self-employment was substantially increasing, particularly in managerial, administrative and craft-related jobs.

'Dynamism', 'flexibility', 'readiness to innovate' and 'enterprise' became the key words of SME policy. Correspondingly, 'de-regulation' became a major theme of this policy from the outset. The aim of SME policy was to provide a business environment in which the maximum degree of flexibility is left to enterprises and in which risk taking is not stifled by regulation. A complementary aim was specific measures or services to help the creation and development of SMEs, by mobilizing private-sector resources where markets do not function efficiently e.g. relatively inexpensive measures to provide business information and facilitate business co-operation, sponsorship of business innovation centres by large corporations and the stimulation of venture and seed capital resources. These two basic aims informed the SME Action Programme of August 1986.

Finally, SME policy represented a response to the adoption of the Single European Act in February 1986. A central question for the SME Task Force was the impact of the basic aims of that Act on SMEs: the establishment (by 31 December 1992) of a Single European Market without internal frontiers in which there would be free movement of goods, services, capital and people; the strengthening of economic and social cohesion; the development of a common policy for scientific and technological development; the strengthening of the European Monetary System (EMS); the emergency of a European social dimension; and co-ordinated action on the environment. This acceleration of the process of European integration made all the more important the introduction of the impact assessment procedure from 1 June 1986. Every Commission proposal for legislation sent to the Council had to be accompanied by the results of an assessment of its impact on business, and SMEs in particular, and on job creation. This evaluation procedure became a powerful tool in the hands of the SME Task Force in effecting legislative and cultural change within the Commission. Here reduction of the cost burden on SMEs and simplification of legislation and administrative procedures that concern SMEs were main objectives. As we shall see later, the SME Task Force

## Small and Medium Sized Enterprises

was able to make its presence felt particularly in
company law policy, taxation policy and competition
policy. Important areas included the opening up of
public procurement for SMEs, especially new methods of
improving their access to public supplies and works
contracts (such as advance information systems and
provisions for the splitting of large contracts);
transparency of new European technical standards and the
greater flexibility implicit in the EC's 'New Approach'
to technical harmonization, which limits binding
Community legislation to what is required for essential
public-interest requirements (such as health and safety,
and environmental protection), or - where harmonization
of standards is not considered essential - to mutual
recognition of national standards; adapting company law,
where accountancy directives include provisions for
derogations to help SMEs and, from 1 July 1989, it will
be possible for SMEs in different member states to cooperate as partners in the new European Economic
Interest Grouping (EEIG); simplifying the tax
environment of SMEs, notably proposals to carry forward
losses for tax purposes and to simplify methods of
levying VAT; exempting from competition policy rules
agreements of minor importance (to encourage SME co-
operation) and 'know-how' licensing and franchising
agreements; and removal of the obstacles to free
movement for the self-employed and employees, notably
with the directive on the freedom of establishment of
professions which introduces a general system for the
mutual recognition of professional qualifications. The
priorities of the SME Task Force within its own sphere
of action were information (the system of European
Business Information Centres and its proposal for a
documentation and information centre on sub-
contracting), co-operation (the revitalization of the
Business Co-operation Centre (BCC) particularly through
the new instrument of the Business Co-operation Network
(BC-NET)) and data-base development on the
characteristics of SMEs in sectors and the impact of the
Single European Market on them.

Small and Medium Sized Enterprises

## The History of EC Policy for SMEs

Against this background the chronology of SME policy development can be understood. The key events have been as follows.

1.  In 1970 the European Commission presented its Memorandum on Industrial Policy (the Colonna Report) to the European Council. Whilst its comprehensive approach proved too controversial to command acceptance, the need for a SME policy had been identified.

2.  In 1971 the Economic and Social Committee (ECOSOC) initiated a study of the situation of SMEs in the EC. This exercise was the first attempt at highlighting the problems facing SMEs and prompted the Commission to introduce assistance measures.

3.  The Commission established a division for 'small, medium-sized and craft enterprises' which, since 1973, has been assisted by the Business Co-operation Centre with the purpose of helping SMEs to establish co-operation agreements, in accordance with the EC's competition rules. Subsidies were also given to numerous activities of trade associations.

4.  1983 was designated the 'European Year of SMEs and Craft Industry' by the European Parliament. This large-scale initiative strengthened European awareness of SMEs and, in particular, culminated on 9 December in a joint action programme for a Community policy on SMEs, in which the European Parliament, the European Commission and ECOSOC laid down basic policy principles, notably on employment and training.

5.  A Commission Communication of 22 May 1984 and the European Parliament's Resolution of 24 May 1984 agreed in detailing a number of steps to improve the administrative, economic and legal climate of SMEs.

Small and Medium Sized Enterprises

6.    In 1985-6 the European Council became active.  The
      turning point was the Brussels summit (March 1985)
      at which four fields for priority action were
      identified, including encouragement of the
      formation and development of SMEs.  Since then the
      European Council has underlined the importance of
      promoting SMEs.  The Luxembourg summit (December
      1985) laid emphasis on the paramount need for
      joint action to improve the environment in which
      firms operate, especially SMEs.  At the Hague
      summit (June 1986) the stress was on a common
      strategy, to be discussed with both sides of
      industry, to promote the spirit of enterprise,
      encourage job flexibility and help the unemployed
      to return to work - with special emphasis on the
      role of SMEs as major sources of growth and jobs.

7.    In September 1985 the Commission established a
      working party with representatives from all the
      directorates-general (DGs) concerned with SMEs.
      Its report to the Commission in November dealt
      with measures to promote the creation or
      development of firms, simplify regulations and
      provide SMEs with support from Community financial
      instruments.

8.    In January 1986 the Commission made one of its
      members, for the first time, specifically and
      directly responsible for SME policy.  This
      Commissioner, Abel Matutes, became chairman of a
      group of interested Commission officials; its task
      was to devise a policy strategy for SMEs.  Three
      features of that policy strategy were outlined
      early on by Matutes: the EC would use existing
      resources to help provide a new and better service
      for SMEs rather than provide direct subsidies; its
      action would be complementary to that at the
      national level where much policy action remained
      appropriate; and EC policy must be designed
      together with small businessmen and not imposed
      from above (British Business 1986).  Information
      and co-operation were being marked out as the key

areas of EC contribution to SME policy.

9.    In June 1986 an independent SME Task Force was
established within the Commission, with an
economist Alan Mayhew as its director, a staff of
approximately forty and a provisional budget of 30
million ECUs for 1987.

It had four objectives:

1. to co-ordinate all relevant activities within
   the Commission (legal, easing of regulatory
   constraints, financing, services and analysis);

2. to promote the approximation of national and EC
   policies;

3. to establish a system for liaison with
   organizations representing SMEs; and

4. to help with the setting-up, at European level,
   of machinery for solving SMEs' practical
   problems and in particular developing a
   communication and training strategy for SMEs to
   enable them to fulfil their information needs
   and have well-qualified staff.

In essence, the SME Task Force had two
functions: internal co-ordination (overseeing the
interests of SMEs in programmes developed by other
services); and the development of projects within
the framework of a general strategy to improve the
environment in which SMEs operate.  Its approach
to the discharge of these two functions was from
the first structured by the policy guidelines of
Matutes and by the small size of the staff and of
the budget.  In this context, the impact
assessment procedure (see earlier) took on
particular significance in its work.  Its
priorities were further reflected in a study of
the impact of EC legislation on SMEs, completed in
1987.  The emphasis was on legal and

administrative simplification and transparency, notably on codifying Community laws and circulating the legal texts more widely. A further study directed at numerous initiatives at the national level (e.g. compliance cost assessment and the Enterprise and Deregulation Unit in the UK and COMFORM in Belgium) reached two conclusions: that there was a need for a fuller exchange of national experiences and that new structures did not in themselves resolve the problem of administrative burdens on SMEs.

10. On 3 November 1986 the Council of Ministers adopted the SME Action Programme. The caveat was that agreement was subject to approval of individual proposals by the Council, particularly their financial implications. For the first time a coherent framework of guidelines for Community action towards SMEs was defined; a number of projects and actions for both the Community and member states was laid down; and an effort was made to motivate future action not only by the Commission but also by all public-sector and private-sector operators concerned with support from SMEs.

11. In May 1987 the European Parliament's report on the SME Action Programme qualified its approval by pointing out that progress had been too slow. In particular, it called for specific action on company law and taxation to facilitate the creation and development of SMEs; improved opportunities to obtain finance through EC programmes; and measures to help them obtain access to public procurement contracts. The European Parliament also called for a Council of Ministers with responsibility for SMEs, to meet at least once a year to discuss Community policy; the first such Council met informally on 5-6 May 1988 and formally on 7 June 1988.

12. In July 1987 the opinion of ECOSOC expressed two

concerns: that there was not a great enough commitment of finance and staff by the Commission to SME policy (the SME Task Force needed to have its mandate extended beyond purely co-ordination to take in management functions); and that better safeguards were needed to ensure the implementation of the programme in the form of deadlines for each section, according to priority.

13. Between 1986 and 1988 the following important Commission communications appeared: two progress reports on the realization of the objectives of the Community Action Programme for Small and Medium Sized Enterprises, COM(87) 238 and COM(88) 64; a Commission communication on strengthening co-operation between European firms: a response to the 1992 internal market deadline; a Commission communication on the evaluation of the European Information Centres - extension of the project; a Commission communication on simplifying administrative procedures within the Community; and a Commission communication on an enterprise policy for the Community, COM(88) 241.

14. On 30 June 1988 the Council resolution on the improvement of the business environment and action to promote the development of enterprises, especially SMEs in the Community, pressed the Commission to accelerate its work on implementing the action programme. In particular, it underlined the importance of the impact assessment exercise; of simplification of legal and fiscal regulations (notably criticizing the Fourth Company Law Directive); of extending the European Information Centre project; of strengthening business co-operation across frontiers (commending the Business Co-operation Network - BC-NET); and of more intensive SME policy discussions in the Council. The Council resolution also requested a reinforcement of the possibilities offered to SMEs within the framework of the structural funds and of the Community research and development

programmes.

15.    In the interests of greater transparency the Commission published and substantially improved the following:

    1. since December 1985 a monthly newsletter _Euroinfo_, providing the business community with information on EC initiatives that might affect SMEs; and

    2. since 1983 a regularly updated practical handbook on _Operations of the European Community Concerning Small and Medium Sized Enterprises_ (see the 1988 edition).

16.    In January 1989 the second Delors Commission transferred the SME Task Force to form the main nucleus of the new DG XXIII under the Portuguese Commissioner Antonio Cardoso E Cunha. DG XXIII had responsibility for enterprise, distributive trades, tourism and co-operatives. A new task-force was established devoted to 'human resources, education, training and youth'. Reflecting these priorities, in 1989 the Commission launched experimental training schemes for preparing SMEs for Europe 1992.

## The SME Task-Force and the Action Programme

Like the first task-force, the IT Task-Force, the SME Task-Force grew out of DG III (industrial policy) and concern about the international competitiveness of the EC _vis-à-vis_ the United States and Japan. In the case of the IT Task-Force the Council was above all worried about the EC's 'technological lag' and wanted to find a new light, flexible structure to collaborate with Europe's 'flagship' companies, such as Philips, Siemens, CGE and Thomson, to develop programmes like ESPRIT. The SME Task-Force was, by contrast, a response to concern about the relatively low rate of job creation in the EC and recognition that small businesses played a major role in the American and Japanese economies.  It was to help the EC develop a more flexible economy based on innovative companies and thus to contribute to the Community's growth and employment strategy.  Internal political dynamics were also at work.  When in 1986 Spain and Portugal joined the EC, the main portfolios within the Commission were already allocated.  The SME Task-Force was a way of enhancing Matutes' responsibilities (he had already been given DG XXIII, co-ordination of the structural funds) and marrying his own business background to the work of the Commission.

The IT Task-Force and the SME Task-Force had a similar political and administrative rationale.  They served to provide profile and visibility to a priority horizontal function cross-cutting the work of the Commission:  and, not being bound by traditional hierarchy, and the requirements of reporting to a director general, they could operate autonomously and plug into the work of the Commission directly at the relevant point.  Also, the careers of the two task-forces seem to suggest that a task-force is a preliminary stage on the route to becoming a new directorate general.  In effect the IT Task-Force became a law unto itself with respect to DG III and eventually took over DG XIII, whilst the SME Task-Force formed the nucleus of the new DG XXIII in 1989.

Here, however, the similarities end.  The IT Task-Force grew bigger than its 'mother' DG (III), had a staff ten times larger than the SME Task-Force and was responsible for big spending programmes.  It had two main relationships to handle within the Commission - DG III and DG XIII.  By contrast, the power of the SME Task-Force was essentially 'the power to persuade'; it had 'many tasks, but little force'.  Its simple, light and open structure mirrored its philosophy; flexibility and an entrepreneurial approach were the characteristics sought by its director, Alan Mayhew.  Hence the SME Task-Force had just three small units: policy and co-ordination; information and relations with Parliament and organizations; and specific services (in particular the European Business Information Centres and the BC-

Small and Medium Sized Enterprises

NET). Externally, its horizontal links were complex and included:

DG III     particularly on the Single European Market programme, on opening up public procurement contracts and on specific sectors;

DG V      for training and for local employment initiatives, including links to CEDEFOP (the European Centre for the Development of Vocational Training) in Berlin;

DG XVI    for regional policy (especially the development of 'indigenous development potential' through Community Programmes) and including the Business and Innovation Centres (and the European Business and Innovation Centre Network, EBN, supporting them) and the joint Europartenariat scheme;

DG IV     for competition policy, notably protection of SMEs from the effects of restrictive agreements and abuses of dominant positions by large firms as well as exemptions for SMEs from competition rules where certain criteria are met;

DG VI     for rural development policy;

DG XII    for basic research programmes like BRITE;

DG XIII   for research and development programmes (ESPRIT, RACE, DELTA etc) and for innovation and technology transfer (notably the SPRINT programme and the activities of the European Association for the Transfer of Technologies, Innovation and Industrial Information, TII);

DG XV     for taxation and company law; and

DG XVIII for financial engineering.

   The SME Task-Force had, from the outset, to live with

the reality that financial power resided elsewhere (notably DG V and DG XVI), that some directorates general insisted on autonomy in their operations (e.g. DG VI in developing the Commission communication of October 1988 on the future of rural society) and that factors of bureaucratic interest generated competition and conflict in other areas (e.g. with the European Business and Innovation Centre Network). Against the background of interest and commitment expressed by the Council, Commission and Parliament, directorates general could be expected to 'play the game' of SME policy. At the same time initial scepticism and self-interest threatened to lead to little more than formal obesiance, ritual responses of support within the Commission that were more symbolic gestures than of practical significance. In this respect the impact assessment exercise (operative from 1 June 1986) because the crucial tool of the SME Task-Force in making its presence felt within the Commission. In order to eliminate unnecessary burdens on SMEs, a directorate general had to submit with each new proposal a form showing its impact on enterprise and on employment. The impact assessment exercise had two functions: as an early-warning system on measures likely to affect SMEs; and as a learning device, focusing the minds of the different directorates general on the problems and needs of SMEs. At first directorates general tended to submit their impact assessment as a formality at the last minute. The great achievement of the SME Task-Force was to take on some key proposals and to win: in particular, DG XI (an environmental policy proposal was blocked because of the demands that it made on SMEs) and DG XV on company law. As directorates general learnt that they could be blocked if they did not co-ordinate at an early stage with the SME Task-Force, so the impact assessment exercise became a central characteristic of EC legislation, for instance in the first concrete manifestation of the 'social dimension' of the European Single Market. Approved by the EC Council of Ministers on 16 December 1988, the framework directive on health and safety of workers at the workplace establishes the principle of the employer's responsibility and sets out the minimum health and safety requirements to be met by companies. It also provides for simplified procedures for SMEs.

The focus of the activities of the SME Task-Force was provided by the SME Action Programme of 1986. Two keywords or principles were complementarity and synergy. The Action Programme was designed to add a European dimension to SME policy and not to substitute for or interfere with the actions of member states; and it was based on the need to develop synergy both between the individual actions of each member state and those that are specifically at the Community level and by close co-operation with organizations representing SMEs. In this important respect the SME Task-Force limited its field of vision, focused its activities and made its tasks more manageable in political and administrative terms. A third principle was to avoid a policy of subsidy to enterprises. The Action Programme groups thirteen projects under two main objectives; each project in turn consists of a series of actions, either at EC or member state level. From these projects it was clear that the European Commission saw a central role for itself as an effective organizer of networks that SMEs can use to pursue their own objectives.

Objective One: improvement of the environment for the creation and development of SMEs within the Community's internal market. This objective is reflected in seven projects that involve major regulatory and administrative actions, particularly within the framework of the Single European Market programme.

1. Promoting the Spirit of Enterprise. Action must concentrate on European training programmes aimed at making the social and cultural climate more propitious for SMEs. A 'SME mentality' must be encouraged in secondary and vocational training schools and universities. COMETT, EUROTECNET and DELTA are examples of such initiatives. It was also increasingly noted that managers of SMEs displayed a certain lack of motivation for training: hence the

management training initiative of 1989.

2.  Improving the Administrative Environment.  Action
    had to ensure that regulation was kept to what was
    strictly necessary; in relative terms, the costs
    fall more heavily on SMEs (they face substantial
    fixed costs and must allocate a greater share of
    their budget and their time).  The means adopted
    included the impact assessment procedure (see
    earlier); efforts to simplify Community legislation
    so that the obligations of SMEs under Community law
    could be more readily identified; and, by an
    exchange of national experiences, encouragement of
    new steps to eliminate obstacles to SMEs and cut
    their costs at the national level.  In particular,
    it was noted that measures were needed chiefly at
    the national level to enhance business
    competitiveness.

3.  Monitoring the Completion of the Internal Market.
    The elimination of barriers to intra-Community trade
    and access to a large internal market of 320 million
    consumers represent a major stimulant to SMEs.  Thus
    the effects of physical barriers, with their
    attendant delays, and administrative and transport
    costs are particularly felt by SMEs.  For large
    firms, frontier formalities are only one cost item;
    for SMEs they often render the frontiers impassible.
    Simplification of customs procedures, with the
    Single Administrative Document (SAD) replacing in
    1988 what were earlier some seventy different forms,
    is of direct benefit to SMEs.  Greater flexibility
    over harmonization of technical standards also helps
    SMEs in reducing the burden of regulation.  The new
    strategy on standards is based less on the
    formulation of detailed harmonized specifications
    than the principle of mutual recognition of national
    rules.  Additionally, the opening up of public
    procurement contracts promises improved business
    prospects for SMEs.  At the same time special action
    is needed to enable SMEs to benefit fully from these
    new possibilities.  In the case of standards both

the process of drawing up specifications in the standardization bodies and the final legal position must be made transparent to SMEs. It is also essential to help SMEs overcome the difficulties that they face in bidding successfully for public works contracts and public supply contracts. Action is required to provide more widely distributed advance information on the purchasing programmes of central and local government bodies; to simplify invitations to tender in the interests of improved access to bidding and greater transparency; and to encourage public contracts exchanges in frontier regions. Under the public works directive, the files relating to costs will have to specify the market share eventually sub-contracted to SMEs. Japanese and American measures that, directly or indirectly, favour SMEs in public procurement policy have been held up as a model.

4. Adapting Company Law. Action must be taken to provide special treatment for SMEs in EC company law. Of particular importance have been: the regulation on the European Economic Interest Grouping (applicable from 1 July 1989) which aims to encourage co-operation between SMEs in different member states (a publicity campaign was planned); the accountancy directives which include provisions for derogations to help SMEs; and the Commission's 1988 proposal for a Twelfth Council directive on company law relating to single-member private limited companies.

5. Adapting Competition Law. Action is designed to facilitate business co-operation involving SMEs. Thus, since 1979, the Commission has made it clear, by means of a general communication directed at small businesses in particular, that sub-contracting agreements are normally not within the scope of Article 85 of the EC Treaty (anti-competitive agreements). In 1986 the Commission extended its definition of agreements of minor importance which, in general, do not warrant an application of Article

85. Also of direct relevance to SMEs are several block exemption regulations, which provide a blanket exemption from the prohibition of anti-competitive agreements if certain conditions are met. Finally, when examining state aid for SMEs, particularly in less-favoured regions, it has been possible to accelerate approval for assistance of 'limited impact' by using simplified procedures.

6. <u>Improving the Tax Environment</u>. The following three Commission proposals were particularly relevant to the needs of SMEs: for a directive on setting up an arbitration procedure to eliminate double taxation affecting firms operating on a cross-frontier basis; for a directive on the carrying forward of losses for tax purposes in order to improve the cash flow and self-financing capacity of SMEs; and for an amendment to the Sixth Directive on simplified methods of collecting VAT and a more realistic exemption arrangement that takes account of the cost of collection. Also, the Commission has made it clear that it does not object to member states having specific tax incentives for SMEs, as long as these incentives comply with the provisions of Article 92 of the EC Treaty (i.e. do not cause any distortions of competition which affect trade between member states).

7. <u>Improving the Social Environment of SMEs</u>. Action here has two dimensions; ensuring that the EC's own social legislation does not increase the cost burden on SMEs; and creating a more favourable legal, tax, social and administrative framework for the creation of producer and service co-operatives. The role of co-operatives in SME policy is specifically underlined.

<u>Objective Two: a positive contribution to the SMEs' needs in terms of flexibility and the provision of capital</u>. This objective is expressed in six projects intended to provide direct help for the creation and

development of SMEs in three ways: by use of EC finance; by introducing a special SME dimension to existing EC activities; and by stimulating the transfer of experience.

1.  <u>Training</u>.  The European Social Fund's schemes must focus on supporting SMEs in their efforts to adapt to new technologies by means of management and production training.  Notable here are COMETT, DELTA and EUROTECNET.

2.  <u>Information</u>.  Crucial to the success of SMEs is the availability of information on markets, products, standards, sources of finance and technological opportunities; and crucial to the success of SME policy is improved statistics so that their needs and problems can be rapidly assessed.  In order to provide such a two-way flow of information the SME Task-Force embarked on a pilot phase to test European Business Information Centres; in 1988 it was decided after an evaluation to extend the scheme across the whole of the EC.  These centres are located in existing 'host' organizations that have close contacts with SMEs.  As well as being equipped with a computer-based system which will respond to requests for information (e.g. on EC programmes and the internal market), the European Business Information Centres will help guide firms towards further co-operation (e.g. in BC-NET).  The SME Task-Force has also worked with the EC Statistical Office in developing data on SMEs by sector and overtime in order to achieve a clearer picture of their experience as a basis for policy making.

3.  <u>Exports</u>.  In order to facilitate SMEs' access to markets in non-member countries the Commission has sought to promote training, joint promotion, market research surveys and information.  Thus, since 1983, the Commission has been developing the General Export Promotion Programme with the aim of organizing joint trade fairs, trade missions, technical seminars and market studies, in

collaboration with the national export promotion organizations of the member states. Since 1979 the Commission has organized a number of pilot schemes to encourage EC exports to Japan (e.g. short-term and long-term visits, sectoral studies, commercial missions); for the period 1987-9 it co-financed the EC/Japan Industrial Co-operation Centre to provide **SMEs** with practical information on Japanese **managerial** and industrial techniques. Also, the Centre for the Development of Industry (CDI), established in 1977 under the Lomé Convention, assists SMEs in establishing new co-operation **agreements** in the sixty-six African, Caribbean and Pacific (ACP) countries.

4. <u>Encouraging New Firms and Innovation</u>. Action was to include the extension and integration of both local employment initiatives (assisted by ELISE) and European Business and Innovation Centres (assisted by the EBN). Links between universities and SMEs in the field of continuing education and training were to be strengthened under the COMETT programme. Measures were also needed to increase SME participation in the EC's research and development programmes (e.g. ESPRIT and BRITE). In particular, the SPRINT programme was seen as a central means of stimulating innovation and technology transfer by encouraging the establishment of networks of advisory bodies for SMEs and by promoting cross-border co-operation on technology and innovation between SMEs.

5. <u>Co-operation between Firms and Regions</u>. Priority was given to the establishment of the computerized Business Co-operation Network (BC-NET) to speed up technical, commercial, financial or sub-contracting co-operation between firms on an interregional and cross-border scale. The Commission had also to consider its role in promoting sub-contracting arrangements and partnerships between large firms and SMEs, with Japan again as a model. In addition, new types of action were required to help promote

co-operation amongst SMEs in less-favoured regions: here a major development involved collaboration of DG XVI and the SME Task-Force in the Europartenariat, first launched in 1988.

6. <u>Provision of Capital</u>. If SMEs were to operate on a European scale, they needed measures to facilitate their access to finance. In particular, Community global loans have been increasingly used to channel financial assistance to SMEs through three main sources; the European Investment Bank (EBI) reserves the major share of its global loans for SMEs (amounting to approval of a total of 595 million ECUs in 1986 compared to 54 million ECUs in 1977); the European Coal and Steel Community (ECSC) loans which aim to redevelop the coal and steel regions and which significantly help SMEs; and the New Community Instrument (NCI) loans for which SMEs can apply since 1982. NCI IV, approved in March 1987, exclusively allocated 750 million ECUs to SMEs; the EBI agreed to make an equivalent amount available to them under the same conditions. Measures were also required to promote venture capital and secondary markets for SMEs. The Commission's major partner in these efforts was the European Venture Capital Association (EVCA), notably in the pilot project 'Venture consort'. The aim was to increase finance for SMEs involved in new technologies at the first stage of capital formation. Attention shifted later to the issue of 'seed' capital. Also, the Commission helped with the start-up of the European Financial Engineering Company (EUROCOFIN) to provide support for transnational co-operation between SMEs.

## Implementing the Action Programme 1986-8

The most striking characteristic of the work of the SME Task-Force and the process of implementing the SME Action Programme was the tension between a clear coherent ideology and set of objectives, on the one hand, and the structural and programmatic complexity and diversity of SME policy, on the other. Its work was driven by the esprit de corps of a highly dedicated and motivated team whose vigour was able to attract external interest within the Commission. A consequence was the emergence of a 'policy community', sharing a common interest in SME policy. The SME Task-Force was to be described as 'experts in sub-contracting', meaning that a group of officials across the Commission, perhaps as large as the number of staff in the Task-Force, became actively involved in supporting its work. This policy community involved in turn a range of networks, dedicated to specific policy issues and indispensible in the achievement of a process of cultural change towards enterprise values across the Commission. Given the freedom of manoeuvre of its title and structure, the SME Task-Force was born a 'missionary' organization with a sense of having two to three years before the conventions of bureaucratization became ascendent.

The ideology motivating the SME Task-Force combined the business experience of the responsible Commissioner, Abel Matutes, and the analytical economic approach of the director of the Task-Force, Alan Mayhew. Matutes articulated the concept of a 'Europe of enterprises'; enterprise was to be seen as the fundamental institution for Europe's economic and social progress. It was opposed to 'the excess of paternalism' and 'obsession with security' that had gripped the EC over previous decades. A 'second-generation Europe' was being inaugurated by the Single European Market and by a new era of rapid technological change that was accelerating the obsolescence of products and production processes. The EC must be equipped for an 'era of action' in which speed and flexibility were essential. Amongst its three preoccupations of employment, competitiveness and enterprise, priority must be given to enterprise. Only competitiveness ensures employment; and only dynamic innovative enterprise ensures competitiveness. The necessary flexibility and speed could be best guaranteed by measures to promote SMEs.

Mayhew added to the ideology the insights of the economist into the theoretical basis of business behaviour, allied to a pronounced 'anti-corporatism' that was ready to challenge the all-too collusive links between some trade and professional groups and parts of the Commission. A case in point was the influence of the accountancy profession on the development of EC company law and taxation proposals. At the same time Mayhew brought the qualities of the administrative realist and entrepreneur. His previous cabinet experience had given him knowledge of the politics of the EC bureaucracy, and he was to rapidly emerge as a successful administrative entrepreneur within the Commission. Given the scale and diversity of SME policy and limited resources, Mayhew prioritized action on three main targets: information, co-operation and harmonized data and terminology. The European Commission could make a decisive contribution in addressing the problems of information facing SMEs (e.g. on the scale and incidence of late payments in different EC countries). Here the development of the role of the European Business Information Centres was central as a means not just of diffusing relevant information to SMEs but also of delivering 'value-added' services (e.g. updating seminars and training courses). This provision of information services was in turn complemented by the policy strategy of strengthening business co-operation across frontiers. Here the SME Task-Force could build on the work of the European Business Co-operation Centre, particularly with the BC-NET which is a network of business advisers throughout the Community linked up by a computerized system. Importance was attached to building up close personal contacts and mutual confidence throughout the network, in other words to developing its informal aspects. Finally, harmonization has to be achieved in both terminology (e.g. of sub-contracting) and in data base development so that national and EC policies were based on a framework of common understandings.

Outside this limited framework of its own management functions the SME Task-Force's effective pursuit of its co-ordination function had to depend on two factors: political support to ensure that its role and impact were not marginalized; and its own capacity to work flexibly and in an entrepreneurial way. Its role as the

guardian of the Commission's 'SME conscience' depended
for its practical effects on the impact assessment
procedure as a way of reaching across the work of the
Commission and sometimes challenging proposals. A key
achievement of the SME Task-Force was in sensibly
picking a limited number of items to challenge and in
winning its way (notably with DG XV over company law
reform). Success in winning Commission battles bred
credibility.

The political climate within which the SME Task-Force
operated was complex and ambiguous. On the one hand,
SME policy enjoyed widespread support across the
political spectrum, in particular within the European
Parliament - from the Italian Communists to the British
Conservatives. For southern European countries, SMEs
were a major fact of economic life; for West Germany,
'Mittelstand' policy represented a long-standing
political consensus about the social as well as economic
need to support a whole way of life with its fostering
of the civic virtues of self-discipline and duty; for
France, and for social democrats and liberals across the
EC countries, SMEs were recognized as the most effective
means of compensating for 'de-industrialization' as the
large manufacturing enterprises shed labour at an
accelerating rate; whilst for 'neo-liberals', and the
British Conservatives in particular, SMEs were the
foremost expression of a new spirit of individualism and
enterprise to be unleashed by deregulation. This
breadth of political support, represented in the SME
Intergroup within the European Parliament, greatly
facilitated the role of the SME Task-Force from 1986
onwards and formed an indispensable backcloth to its
success in engineering cultural change within the
Commission.

On the other hand, this policy consensus masked a
heritage of different approaches to SMEs. The social
dimension of SME policy was notably pronounced in
southern Europe where a key role was assigned to co-
operatives (notably in Italy) and in Ireland where
community business was especially strong; Belgium and
France gave particular prominence to SME training in
areas affected by coal, iron and steel closures (e.g.

the Intercommunal Training Association in Le Bruaysis, Nord Pas-de-Calais, and the Communal Committee for Employment in Genk, Belgium), for social as well as economic reasons; whilst the ideological context of a newly resurgent SME policy in the UK was 'enterprise culture' and rewards for individual effort and achievement. Reflecting the ideologies of its Commissioner and director the SME Task-Force gravitated more towards the 'enterprise culture' end of the spectrum. West German 'Mittelstand' policy became the symbol of the worst aspects of SME policy within the EC; protectionist and defensive in approach, this policy seemed to encourage a form of 'corporatism' in which opportunities for new entrants and therefore competition was denied in the name of high standards of health, safety and product quality. The SME Task-Force became embroiled in controversy not just with the Chamber of German Industry and Commerce but also within the Commission where the President Jacques Delors argued the case for an 'economie sociale' in SME policy (in practical terms a reference to the need to build up the training dimension).

This ideological and political background provides a necessary but far from sufficient background for understanding how the SME policy of the Commission was implemented and evolved from 1986 to 1988. It helps us to understand the 'rules of the game' of SME policy at the EC level, the factors guiding the behaviour of the actors towards each other and influencing how they used their resources. As far as the SME Task-Force and its policy community was concerned, these rules included norms about the acceptable and unacceptable uses of EC authority, the proper language in which to express policy, an emphasis on informality, an expectation of consultation, and the pursuit of mutual advantages and benefits within the various policy networks. At the same time this ideological and political background does not adequately help us to understand how in reality SME policy developed after 1986. A gap opened between the 'rhetoric' of the SME Action Programme and the reality of the policy process. One explanation of this change can be dismissed at the outset. There is a well-documented tendency in industrial policy development for agencies to become increasingly identified with their client group over time. This phenomenon of 'agency capture' or 'clientelism' did not occur in the case of the SME Task-Force. An important aspect of its operation was the absence of a strong associational structure representing SMEs (e.g. the European Organization for Medium and Small Undertakings, EMSU, or the European Confederation for Independent Workers, CEDI). In practice, it was pressurizing the key EC associations representing small employers, the retail trade and chambers of commerce for their members to lobby at the <u>national</u> level for greater priority to the needs and interests of SMEs. The SME Task-Force moved ahead of the traditional associational groups like chambers of commerce in developing SME policy and was able to maintain a relative freedom of manoeuvre compared to many directorates general which remained locked in clientelist relations. In seeking out a new constituency in this way and challenging old attitudes and relationships the SME Task-Force retained a significant capability to shift its own ground (an exception was the field of venture capital where the development of EC policy was restrained by the industry lobby). The EC budget has in fact an item (6421) enabling the Commission to grant aid to organizations bringing together or representing SMEs.

During this period a learning process took place about the nature of the SME constituency that led to some tension between the theory and the practice of policy. In theory, the SME Task-Force was there to help all SMEs, thus encompassing an enormous range of companies. This function continued to be performed, for instance in the fields of company law and taxation. In practice, however, the SME Task-Force came to recognize that some SMEs (a small minority) are more likely to use its services and deserve its support than others, in particular medium-sized companies which had on the whole a greater capability to extend across EC borders. At the level of policy norms this learning process was demonstrated in the commitment by 1988 to an enterprise policy of fostering competitiveness. An EC enterprise policy involved helping firms that wanted to grow across borders, whether they were larger or smaller in size. A role of assisting all SMEs in general policy measures of deregulation or tax exemption remained critical. At the same time such mechanisms as BC-NET, the European Business Information Centres, DG XIII's SPRINT programme and DG XVI's EBN sorted out the enterprising companies from the others - the innovative people with good ideas about market, technology, finance and training, with a positive, forward-looking and outward-looking approach and with the capability of developing a sound business plan. Proposals for management training for SMEs were an attempt to widen the scope of enterprising companies within the EC; training was, after all, a demonstration of willingness to invest in growth. It remained the case, nevertheless, that the SME Task-Force had learnt that it was more cost-effective to deal with medium sized companies. This rule was not expressed in formal policy; it found its expression in behaviour.

## Prospects for SME Policy After 1988

Following a major phase of policy innovation and of cultural change within the European Commission, by 1989 the SME policy of the European Community was entering a new phase of consolidation and realism. Directorate-general status could be interpreted either as a sign of maturity and success or as an omen of lost vigour and bureaucratization. Also, the title and responsibilities of DG XXIII represented a change of policy formula: 'enterprise' was, for instance, brought together with artisans, commerce, distributive trades and tourism. The cumulative impacts of these small changes could turn out to be more significant than at first realised, not least as the new directorate general trespassed more on the grounds of other DGs. There would be new battles to fight within the Commission on a wider and more complex front; the identity of SME policy would be less clearly defined.

A number of policy changes were becoming apparent. BC-NET and the European Business Information Centres had still to be completed. More significantly, the concept of enterprise was drawing attention to the important catalytic role of large companies, notably multinationals, in the field of SMEs e.g. by encouragement of sub-contracting, corporate venturing and management buy-outs. Greater emphasis was being placed on opening up new possibilities for SMEs in European sub-contracting by tougher contract requirements and earlier information: this issue was taken up by DG III in 1989. Further developments to be considered in the next section include a shift of concern from venture capital to seed capital provision; an interest in the 'value added' services that can be delivered through the European Business Information Centres; the theme of management training for SMEs; a re-orientation of priorities within the European Business and Innovation Centre Network (EBN); and a new prominence to the role of SMEs in rural development (witness the proposed NCI V, the Future of Rural Society communication from the Commission and the European Parliament's resolution on restructuring the European Agricultural Guidance and Guarantee Fund).

Over the period 1986-8 the role of the SME Task-Force in inducing cultural change within the European Commission must not be underestimated. Its very approach was distinctive: based not on the traditional Commission fixation on the legal basis for action and on committing the resources allocated but on monitoring and evaluating Commission proposals and programmes with reference to their impacts on SMEs. The SME dimension began to be increasingly recognized across EC programmes, from research and development through competition to tax and company law. Also, during the same period, the SME Task-Force, and other parts of the Commission, abandoned a somewhat intellectual approach to SMEs in favour of a greater realism about enterprise and about the scale and complexity of the SME sector. Specialized, high-quality companies with a strong commitment to market share, sales and profitability and to innovation are likely to be at the forefront of those helped by the EC's SME policy (e.g. through co-operation agreements) to take advantage of the greater export opportunities opened up by the Single European Market. At the same time small companies tend to be preoccupied with specific internal problems rather than external issues and lack the internal capability (expertise, resources and time) to commit people to researching the European market dimension: many are the product of labour shedding by large firms and represent 'forced' entrepreneurship: and, in a large number of cases, where companies have been formed to enjoy the benefits of a 'life style' of independence and self-reliance, even the interest in accessing EC programmes may be lacking. The major lesson is that certain kinds of specialized, high quality companies can most readily benefit from the various networks developed by the Commission (e.g under the SPRINT and BC-NET programmes); the latter companies stand to gain more directly from the support measures of the Commission. In this respect the EC's SME policy is just emerging from its infancy, from a naive faith in the virtues of encouraging people to start their own businesses towards attention to the deeper problems of lack of competitiveness and of encouraging greater demand to participate in European networks (e.g. through training programmes).

## FURTHER READING

P. Burns and J. Dewhurst, <u>Small Business in Europe,</u> Macmillan, 1986.

P. Burns and A. Kippenberger, <u>Entrepreneur: Eight British Success Stories of the 1980s</u>, Macmillan, London, 1988.

Commission of the European Communities, <u>An Enterprise Policy for the Community</u>, COM (88) 241/2 final, 10th May 1988.

Commission of the European Communities, <u>Europe 1992: Developing an Active Company Approach to the European Market</u>, 1988.

Commission of the European Communities, <u>Improving Competitiveness and Industrial Structures in the Community,</u> EC, Luxembourg, 1987.

Commission of the European Communities, <u>Operations of The European Community Concerning Small and Medium Sized Enterprises: Practical Handbook</u>, 1988 edition, SME Task-Force, 1988.

Commission of the European Communities, <u>Report by the Commission to the Council on the Realization of the Objectives of the Community Action Programme for Small and Medium Sized Enterprises</u>, COM (87) 238 final, EC, Brussels.

Small and Medium Sized Enterprises

Commission of the European Communities, Second Report by the Commission on the Realization of the Objectives of the Community Action Programme for Small and Medium Sized Enterprises, COM (88) 64 final. EC, Brussels.

Commission of the European Communities, Simplifying Administrative Procedures within the Community. General Considerations. COM (88) 404 final, EC, Brussels.

Commission of the European Communities, Towards a European Technology Community, COM(85) 84 and COM(85) 530 final, EC, Brussels.

Commission of the European Communities, 22nd General Report on the Activities of the European Communities, EC, Luxembourg, 1989.

S. Crossick, 'Comparative Assessment of the Impact of 1992 on SMEs and MNCs', European Affairs, 1988, no 3, pp 83-95.

J. Curran, Small Firms and their Environments, Small Business Research Unit, Kingston Polytechnic, London, 1987.

I. Drexel, Vocational Training Problems in Small and Medium Sized Enterprises, EC, Luxembourg, 1986.

ELISE, The 1989 Directory of Local Development Agencies, Brussels.

M. Lazerson, 'Organizational Growth of Small Firms', American Sociological Review, 1988, vol 53.

## Small and Medium Sized Enterprises

Les P.M.E. Dans Les Systèmes Économiques Contemporains, Association Internationale de Droit Economique, Brussels, 1986.


S. E. Lloyd and S. Pratt (eds), Guide to European Venture Capital Sources, 2nd edition, Venture Economics, 1988.


D.A. Pinder, 'Small Firms, Regional Development and the European Investment Bank', Journal of Common Market Studies, 1986, no 3, pp 171-86.


A. Rajan, Services - The Second Industrial Revolution? Butterworths, London, 1987.


H. Roos and W. Bos (eds), Small and Medium Sized Enterprises: Keystone for a Free and Prosperous Europe, Tilburg University Press, 1986.


R. Stobaugh and L. T. Wells (eds), Technology Crossing Borders, HBS Press, 1984.


D.J. Storey and S.G. Johnson, Job Creation in Small and Medium Sized Enterprises, EC, Luxembourg, 1987.


D. Storey, The Performance of Small Firms, Croom Helm, 1987.

**APPENDIX**

1. SME Task-Force (1988)

   Commissioner - Abel Matutes
   Director - Alan Mayhew

   **Unit 1**    Policy and Co-ordination
   **Unit 2**    Information and Relations with Business
                 Organizations and the European Parliament
                 European Information
   **Unit 3**    Implementation :

        a.    European Information Centres
        b.    BCC and BC-NET

2. DG XXIII (proposed structure May 1989)

   Director-General - not appointed

   1. Directorate for Enterprise Policy (Director:
      Alan Mayhew) - incorporating the old SME Task-
      Force and including the unit dealing with
      social economy (i.e. management training)

   2. Directorate for Commerce, Retail Trade and
      Distribution, and Tourism (no director
      appointed, de facto Mayhew discharges this
      role).

   Address:   80 rue d'Arlon
              1040 Brussels
              Tel: (02) 236 16 76

**SECTION II**
**SUMMARIES OF KEY EUROPEAN COMMUNITY PROGRAMMES ON SMEs**

# PROMOTING EXTERNAL BUSINESS AND TRADE

## Community's General Export Promotion Programme

This programme has been developing since 1983 and aims to target specific markets where Community promotion can facilitate market access and trade development by EC companies. Close co-operation with the export promotion agencies of the Member States is pursued through the Trade Promotion Group where their representatives agree specific action under the chairmanship of DG I (External Relations). Targets have been: Japan, Brunei, China, Indonesia, Malaysia, Philippines, Singapore, South Korea and Thailand. A co-ordinated programme is updated twice annually and involves co-subsidy from the Commission and from the national export promotion agencies. The four major activities supported are:

1. Trade Fairs. Exhibitors receive financial assistance (towards costs of exhibition space and design) and are supported by a Commission information stand and publicity if they exhibit together in an EC pavilion under EC colours.

2. Trade Missions. Where it can be demonstrated that EC firms enjoy a comparative advantage over competitors, sectoral missions can be supported.

3. Market Studies. National export promotion agencies will make available sectoral and public purchasing studies.

4. Technical Seminars. Seminars can be sponsored when they promote new developments in EC technologies.

Small and Medium Sized Enterprises

Technical seminars in particular have been specifically directed at SMEs which can also expect to benefit from the whole range of these activities.
   Commission Contact:  DG I/C/3, 1 Avenue Cortenberg, B-1040 Brussels, tel: (02) 235 49 58.
   In 1989 DG I/C/3 is publishing guides on exporting for SMEs: tel: (02) 236 03 62.


**Exports to Japan**

   This programme has been developing since 1979 and aims to encourage EC firms, especially SMEs, to export to Japan.   Of the five activities promoted by the European Commission, the most important is the Training Programme in Japan for Young Community Executives.   By the end of the ninth training programme (ETP9) in December 1990 nearly 300 places will have been awarded on the long-term, 18-month programme; fifty-two in ETP9. 80% of the young trainees who took part in previous ETPs now work for EC firms in Japan or EC export services to Japan.   The objective is to form a reserve of EC executives capable of successfully handling their firms' business relations with Japan.   A greater number of participants from SMEs has been noticeable, across a spread of industrial and commercial sectors.   The programme involves a one-year intensive language course in Japanese, followed by a six-month period of on-the-job training in selected Japanese companies, and a parallel programme of conferences and seminars. Participants must be between 25 and 35 years of age and have received a university-level education or equivalent.   They must be citizens of an EC country and be employed by EC firms oriented towards export and interested in the Japanese market.   The trainees receive a monthly allowance.  Language classes and costs related to the programme are paid for by the Commission.  Firms must seek to ensure that trainees are later employed in a post that is actively involved in export business to Japan.   The Commission contact is: DG I/F/1, Division Japan, 200 rue de la Loi, B-1049 Brussels, tel: (02) 235 40 91.

Small and Medium Sized Enterprises

Short-Term Visits to Japan. This programme comprises two trips a year of three weeks duration and is organized and financed by the Japanese External Trade Organization (JETRO). Of the fifteen to twenty EC executives normally involved, some ten are selected by the Commission. The Commission contact is: DG I/F/1, tel: (02) 235 40 73.

Sectoral Measures. The EC undertakes sectoral market studies (available free of charge e.g. ceramics, beverages, milk products, electrical household goods, advanced medical materials) and helps to finance commercial missions (where firms come from a representative selection of EC states and normally have the support of EC industrial federations). The Commission contact is: DG I/F/1, tel: (02) 235 82 28.

General Action. The Commission may subsidize courses for senior executives on Japanese markets and sponsor study trips to Japan on specific themes (e.g. technology transfer). It also publishes a list of EC companies operating in Japan that are prepared to help SMEs enter the Japanese market and monitors calls for public tender in Japan (made available through the 'S' series of the Official Journal and its computerized equivalent TED). The Commission contact is: DG I/F/1, tel: (02) 235 45 84.

EC/Japan Industrial Co-operation Centre. The objective of this pilot action (June 1987 - March 1989), is to provide businessmen and engineers from SMEs with practical information on Japanese industrial management and engineering techniques. The scheme is co-financed by the Commission and by Japan's MITI (Ministry for International Trade and Industry), and firms are expected to pay travel and accommodation costs. The Industrial Co-operation Centre provides information services on establishing companies in Japan or funding partners for joint ventures; and offers professional training for, on average, four to six months in Japan. The Commission contact is: DG III (Internal Market and Industrial Affairs), 200 rue de la Loi, B-1049 Brussels, tel: (02) 235 86 15.

Small and Medium Sized Enterprises

## Project Opportunities in the Mediterranean Countries

Co-operation agreements with a number of Mediterranean countries cover trade and financial matters (notably free or favourable access for certain products to the EC markets) and open up opportunities for companies, including SMEs, to tender for infrastructural, industrial, energy, agricultural and training projects. These agreements last for an indefinite period and contain five-year renewable financial protocols which define the overall amount of EC aid and how it is to be provided. Under the third financial protocols (1987-92) there is a considerable increase of overall allocation (to take account of inflation) and provision for a maximum of 2% interest subsidy on European Investment Bank (EIB) loans and a fixed amount of risk capital as well as grant aid from the EC budget. Co-operation agreements exist with three groups of countries:

1. Maghreb - Algeria, Morocco and Tunisia
2. Mashraq - Egypt, Jordan, Lebanon, Syria
3. Others - Cyprus, Israel (of limited scope), Malta, Turkey and Yugoslavia.

Support is particularly directed at infrastructural schemes (e.g. water supply and road construction projects), industrial projects for SMEs, rural development projects, technical co-operation schemes in research and training (e.g. tourism promotion, water resources), and energy projects. The major recipients under the third protocol are to be (in order of importance) Egypt (with over 25%), Morocco, Algeria and Tunisia. The procedure involves the formulation of individual indicative programmes for each state, followed by joint agreement on a proposal-by-proposal basis of a financing agreement. Advanced information about projects going out to tender can be gained from:

1. the Mediterranean countries' own governments
2. the permanent representations of the Member States to the Community.

3. DG I/G (External Relations): for general introduction
   and names and members of the desk officers for each
   Mediterranean country, tel: (02) 235 23 85 or (02)
   235 22 12.

EC Budget item 9671 indicates that particular
priority will be given to small businesses. SMEs should
also note the creation of the 'EC International
Investment Partners' as a financial instrument in 1988
to promote investments by EC companies in a series of
Mediterranean, Asian and Latin American developing
countries, in the form of joint ventures with local
companies (notably combined with a transfer of
technology and know-how). The EC acts by co-financing
and solely through existing financial intermediaries.
     In April 1989 the 'Mediterranean' Intergroup of the
European Parliament (having some 100 MEPs as members)
proposed a global co-operation agreement between the EC
and these countries, including the creation of a Council
for Mediterranean Co-operation.

## Project Opportunities in the Asian and Latin American Developing Countries (ALA). Council Regulation 442/81 L48. 28.2.81

Co-operation and financial agreements between the EC
and certain Asian and Latin American countries date from
1976 and are covered by a basic Council regulation of
1981 and by annual guidelines decided by the Council.
The basic regulation gives priority to the poorest
countries (especially the rural sector); regional
projects; and a reserve for post-catastrophe
reconstruction. Aid is in the form of grant aid. The
large majority of the aid goes to Asia e.g. Bangladesh,
Burma, China, India, Indonesia, Laos, Pakistan,
Philippines, Sri Lanka, Thailand, Vietnam; examples of
Latin American countries are Bolivia, Columbia, Costa
Rica, Ecuador, Guatemala, Nicaragua, Paraguay and Peru.
Companies, including SMEs, can win contracts if they
have advanced information and should cultivate close
contacts with the relevant permanent representation of

## Small and Medium Sized Enterprises

their Member State as well as with DG I/H/3 (External
Relations) on economic monitoring and project
identification, tel: (02) 235 13 95 and with DG VIII/5
(Development) on project implementation and technical
assistance tel: (02) 235 13 72. Final information about
projects subject to open tender can be gained from the
'S' series of the Official Journal. See EC Budget item
9315 for encouraging joint ventures and investment in
Latin America, particularly with small businesses, and
item 9305 for Asia.

See also the 'EC International Investment Partners'
instrument under the previous section.

## Project Opportunities Under the Lomé Convention

Since 1975 the EC provides aid under the Lomé
Convention to sixty-six African, Caribbean and Pacific
(ACP) States and the Overseas Territories (OCT) of
France, the Netherlands and Britain. This aid is made
available mainly under the European Development Fund
(EDF), which is administered by DG XVIII and also by
European Investment Bank (EIB) subsidized loans. The
activities are governed by successive five-year
conventions (LOME I 1975-9, LOME II 1979-84 and LOME III
1984-90) and by the principle of co-operation with
individual ACP states in agreeing jointly an indicative
aid programme, followed by individual action programmes
and projects, and a financing proposal. DG VIII is
responsible for ensuring that aided projects are
economically and technically sound and implementation is
effective. Total financial aid under Lome III for
ACP/OCT states was 8,620 million ECUs.

As far as SMEs are concerned, it is important to note
that the Lomé Convention includes an ACP commitment to
create favourable conditions for EC investment and
provides for financial and technical co-operation -
grants, special loans and risk capital financed by EDF
and EIB. They are provided with opportunities to win
contracts for works projects (60% of all projects e.g.
construction contracts), supply projects (20% of all
projects e.g. supplies for agriculture) and service

Small and Medium Sized Enterprises

projects (20% of all projects e.g. feasibility studies, consultancy reports, provision of technical staff). Main priorities are agricultural and rural development, fisheries, industrial development, mining and energy, transport and communication, tourism and vocational training.

Tendering procedures differ significantly:

1. For works and supply projects there are five methods:
   a. international competitive bidding (tender specifications are put out to EC/ACP states with preference given to local firms - 10% for small works contracts and 15% for supplies);
   b. restricted invitation (selected candidates are invited to tender for emergency aid or an urgent operation);
   c. accelerated tenders for small works contracts (publicity is limited to the ACP state itself or its neighbours);
   d. mutual agreement procedures for urgent or small-scale operations (the ACP state selects the contractor/supplier subject to Commission approval); and
   e. contract executed by the ACP authority (where the estimated cost is less than 4 million ECUs).

2. For technical assistance/consultancy firms must first register with DG VIII for contracts financed by EDF by completing a computerized questionnaire. Contracts are awarded either by restricted invitation to tender (chosen from the file) or (for small operations) by a direct proposal of one or two candidates to the ACP state.

   In order to realize the project opportunities under the Lomé Convention SMEs need good contacts and advance information, in particular to:

   a. the ACP national authorizing officer in each ACP state (usually a minister or senior official), responsible for the preparation of tenders and placing of contracts;
   b. the EC Commission's Delegation in the ACP state,

> responsible for ensuring that the terms of the Convention in respect of tendering and contracts procedures are respected;
> c. DG VIII: for consultancy contracts registration, tel: (02) 235 94 17;
> d. the relevant permanent representation of the Member State in Brussels;
> e. the ACP 'Courier' magazine and its equivalent data base (PABLI); and
> f. Official Journal 'S' series and its equivalent data base (TED).

## Business Co-operation Between EC and ACP Firms

The Centre for the Development of Industry (CDI) was established in 1977 under the Lomé Convention and is financed under the EDF with the aim of advancing the industrial development of the ACP states. Its activities are particularly concerned to encourage co-operation between EC and ACP firms in the form of long-term contractual arrangements in the following main ways: by acting as a neutral, experienced mediator in negotiations; and by reducing the promotional, preinvestment and implementation costs of establishing new developments in ACP countries. This assistance is mainly directed to SMEs which meet the following criteria:

1. are active in the priority sectors of ACP countries (agro-food, wood, metal processing, leather, energy, paper and printing, building materials);
2. wish to take equity in a joint venture or to enter into a long-term contractual agreement (e.g. licensing, franchising, sub-contracting) with an ACP partner; and
3. can offer financial guarantees.

The advantages for EC firms are:

1. the prospect of restructuring by transferring labour intensive processes or uncompetitive plant to ACP

countries;
2. access to ACP raw materials, markets and fiscal incentives; and
3. opportunity to expand by exploiting their know-how in an ACP environment.

To benefit from the wide variety of services to SMEs by getting onto its file, contact: CDI, 28 rue de l'Industriè, B-1040 Brussels, tel: (02) 513 41 00.

**PROMOTING SMES WITHIN THE INTERNAL MARKET PROGRAMME**


## The Removal of Physical Barriers

European Commission (1988), 'The Economics of 1992',
European Economy, 35, March, pp46-8.
   This document identifies customs formalities and
resultant paperwork as one of the three major obstacles
to trade (the others are technical regulations and
public procurement practices) and estimates that they
add about 1.5% to 2% to the final cost of products to
the consumer. Three factors have made customs
procedures more complex and burdensome: the need to
handle problems of tax adjustment arising from national
differences in VAT and excise duties; health and
transport regulations; and compliance with bilateral
trade quota regimes. The major component of these costs
are administrative costs, totalling about 7.5 billion
ECUs; costs associated with frontier delays added about
1-2 billion ECUs to this total.
   The cost of customs procedures varied (a) across
industries, with the costs being highest in textiles,
footwear and clothing, paper, mineral oil refining,
rubber products, precision engineering and food; and (b)
from country to country, with Belgium having the most
'open' and Italy the most 'closed' frontier. Of
particular importance to this volume, costs per
consignment could be as much as 30-40% higher for small
firms (less than 250 employees) than for large firms.
   In this latter respect SMEs stand to benefit
disproportionately from the 1992 programme's priority to
the elimination of frontier controls and border checks:
and this, in turn, requires the removal of different
national health and transport standards and the
harmonization of indirect taxes.
   The launch (in January 1988) of the Single
Administrative Document (SAD), to cover all the export,

transit and import documentation needed for EC and many third country exports, was a step towards simplifying export procedures. At the same time it remains a very complicated form (listing details of the exporter, the customer, the goods being shipped and the duties to be paid), whilst other documents are required by banks, shippers and customers (e.g. invoices, certificates of origin, bills of lading, documentary letters of credit, bills of exchange). Attitude and familiarity are important here. SMEs can be put off by customs procedures and export documentation as a bureaucratic chore or nightmare. Alternatively, they can treat exporting as a learning process, in which problems are reduced to routine office procedures or handed to intermediaries like forwarding agents.

COM(84) 749 final: Proposal for a Council Directive on the easing of controls and formalities applicable to nationals of the Member States when crossing intra-Community borders
COM(85) 224 final: Amendment to the proposal
The aim of this proposal is that EC citizens should no longer be obliged to stop when crossing internal Community borders. At the same time it seeks to evolve a system whereby border officials can ascertain that the traveller meets certain conditions and need not be stopped. The details are to be found in the companion volume on the Internal Market by Dr Kevin Featherstone.

COM(86) 524 final: Proposal for a Council Regulation on the abolition of exit formalities at internal Community frontiers - introduction of common border posts
This proposal aims to streamline border formalities by abolishing the remaining administrative checks on leaving a country and replacing them with a single operation at the office of entry into the Member State. For details see the volume by Dr Kevin Featherstone.

Small and Medium Sized Enterprises

The Schengen Group

This group of five EC countries (France, West Germany, Belgium, Luxembourg and the Netherlands) was preparing in 1989 to sign an agreement to abolish their internal border controls in 1990 as a prototype for an EC agreement. The main elements of the agreement were likely to be that common borders can, in principle, be crossed at any point without a border check; that external borders can be crossed only at designated points during specific hours; that uniform visa and asylum policies will be introduced; that visa restrictions will not apply to citizens of EC countries; and that each Member State must be responsible for controlling the reinforced 'ring fence' at the external borders. This agreement is likely to put new pressure on Britain, Ireland and Denmark which have strongly opposed abolishing border controls on the ground that drug traffickers, terrorists and illegal immigrants would benefit.

**Removal of Barriers to Free Movement of Labour and of the Professions**

The General Directive on Higher Education Diplomas

This Directive, adopted by the Internal Market Council on 21 December 1988, aims to make it possible for many professionals - notably accountants, engineers, lawyers, physiotherapists and teachers - to practise in other Member States without having to requalify every time. It will come into force at the beginning of 1991. The Directive is general in scope, applying to all professions which require a diploma acquired after at least three years (or the part-time equivalent) training of university or equivalent level. Its provisions also apply irrespective of whether (as is usual) the professions are publicly regulated or (as in Ireland and Britain) many professions are self-regulated. The condition of mutual recognition and right of establishment is that the education and training of professionals must be 'equivalent' to what is required of the 'host' Member State's own nationals with respect to <u>duration</u> and <u>content</u>.

1. If the duration of education and training required in the 'host' state is longer, the latter may require professionals from other Member States to provide evidence of a professional experience.
2. In the case of the content of education and training not meeting the requirements of the 'host' state, a different procedure applies. In most professions, the migrant will be able to choose between taking an aptitude test covering the areas that have not been studied or undergoing a period of practice under the supervision of a qualified member of the profession. Where the practice of a profession requires a precise knowledge of national law, the 'host' state may itself stipulate whether a migrant should take a test or undergo a period of supervised practice. This Directive has its origins in a Commission proposal of 1985: COM(85) 355 final, as amended COM(86) 257 final.

<u>COM(79) 215: Proposal for a Council Directive on a right of residence for nationals of Member States in the territory of another Member State</u>
<u>COM(85) 292: Amended Proposal</u>
This proposal aims to establish recognition of a right of permanent residence in a Member State for nationals of other Member States over 18 years of age and for members of their families who do not enjoy this right by virtue of EC measures in respect of free movement of employed and self-employed workers. For details see the volume by Dr Kevin Featherstone.

**Removal of Technical Barriers**

<u>Directive 83/189</u>
This Directive seeks to prevent the creation of new technical barriers by requiring Member States to notify in advance the EC Commission of all draft technical

regulations and standards covering industrially manufac-
tured products in order to permit the latter to assess
their compatibility with the principle of the free
movement of goods laid down in Articles 30-36 of the
Treaty of Rome. From 1 January 1989 the scope of the
Directive has been enlarged to effectively cover all
products e.g. foodstuffs, agricultural products and
medicinal products. Commission action to counter such
restrictive measures was given an added legal basis in
two rulings of the European Court of Justice: the Cassis
de Dijon case (1979) and the 'Reinheitsgebot' case
(1987). The Commission receives annually between 500
and 750 complaints from individuals or companies about
possible violations of Articles 30-36. A SME can submit
such a case, preferably supported by a relevant trade
association, for (free) Commission investigation by
contacting DG III/C/1, 200 rue de la Loi, B-1049
Brussels.

**European Commission (1988), 'The Economics of 1992',
European Economy, 35, March, pp44-6 and p53**
This document identifies the costs created by
technical regulations, standards and testing
certification procedures which govern the specification
of goods that can be sold in the various national
markets and which inhibit trade in goods thought likely
to adversely affect the health or safety of consumers in
the various national markets. These barriers seem to be
especially important in food (see the two Court rulings
above), pharmaceuticals, electrical engineering,
mechanical engineering and precision equipment as well
as in metal products, motor vehicles and office and
data-processing machinery. Once again, the costs seem
to weigh more heavily on small than on large firms.

**COM(85) 19 final: Technical harmonization and
standards: A new approach**
The aim of this new approach to harmonization is to
halt the proliferation of excessively technically
detailed product-by-product Directives. In order to

speed progress Directives should encompass wide product categories and types of hazard and be limited to the 'essential' safety requirements or other requirements in the general interest. The task of drafting the detailed technical specifications is entrusted to the main European standards bodies, in particular CEN (the European Committee for Standardization). For details see the volume by Dr Kevin Featherstone.

By March 1989 the following 'New Approach' Directives had been agreed: simple pressure valves (June 1987), toy safety (May 1988) and construction products (December 1988). The Council had also reached provisional agreement, subject to the views of the European Parliament, on the draft electromagnetic compatibility Directive (November 1988) and the draft machinery safety Directive (December 1988). Draft Directives under discussion included personal protective equipment, gas appliances and non-automatic weighing instruments. Further draft Directives for discussion included mobile machinery, lifting equipment and active medical implants.

SMEs should keep in very close contact with their trade association, their national standards authority and the relevant sponsoring government ministry both on the development of the 'New Approach' Directives and for advice on national regulations and practice.

## COM(88) 10: A policy statement on technical specifications, testing and certification: The global approach

In this proposal of November 1988 the European Commission seeks to encourage the use of quality assurance, the use of the European standards for testing laboratories and certification bodies, as well as the development of national accreditation networks; proposes a more systematic approach to the testing and certification requirements of 'New Approach' Directives; and envisages the establishment of a European Organization for Testing and Certification to promote agreements for the mutual recognition of certificates and test results. The aim is a Council of Ministers' Resolution on testing and certification during 1989.

Small and Medium Sized Enterprises

## Opening Up Public Procurement Contracts

European Commission (1988), 'The Economics of 1992', European Economy, 35, March, pp56-60
Public procurement contracts account for over 10% of the EC's GNP, whilst public policy tends to systematically favour domestic over foreign suppliers (often building up 'national champions' e.g. in telecommunications and defence) at the expense of both the taxpayer and the EC's industrial competitiveness. Many SMEs stand to gain from open tendering for works contracts and supply contracts.

Directive 88/295: the new supplies Directive
This Directive came into force on 1 January 1989 and amended Directive 77/62 (which has been already amended in Directive 80/767). The Directive was based on a Commission proposal 86/297, altered twice with 87/233 and 87/468. It strengthened the system of advance information about intended contracts by product area, required the publication of information on the contracts awarded, defined more precisely and restrictively sectoral exemptions, gave preference to European standards, and introduced a new 'negotiated procedure', as well as lowered the threshold at which the Directive applies to contracts.

COM(86) 679 final: Proposal for a Council Directive concerning the co-ordination of procedures for the award of public works contracts
COM(88) 354 final: Amended Proposal
This proposal seeks to amend Directive 71/305 which is seen as having had only a slight impact on the transparency of public works contracts. Less than one quarter of public contracts in the EC were covered by the Directive, and no more than 4-5% of the total value of such contracts has been awarded to EC firms not established in the country in which the invitation to tender was issued. It aims to extend the scope of coverage to contracts involving private companies,

subsidized to more than 50% by public authorities, and to include services related to public works (e.g. design, financing, management); to achieve a stricter definition of what constitutes an exemption and a strict limitation on the use of the 'single-tender ' procedure; to introduce an advance information procedure (six to twelve months ahead); to give preference to European standards; and to raise appreciably the threshold at which open competition comes into operation (but in respect only of publication of notices in the Official Journal). It was also proposed to produce a users' handbook of the provisions governing the opening up of public works contracts in the Community (Official Journal: C358/87). Final adoption of the new Works Directive took place in June 1989.

COM(88) 376: Communication from the Commission on a Community regime for procurement in the excluded sectors: water, energy, transport and telecommunications
This document was followed by proposals for a Council Directive on procurement procedures of entities providing water, energy and transport services (COM(88) 377) and a Council Directive on procurement procedures of entities operating in the telecommunications sector (COM(88) 378). These proposals to apply purchasing rules to hitherto 'excluded sectors' did not encounter fundamental objections (though there was concern about the extent of coverage). In accordance with Directive 88/301 the telecommunications terminal equipment market is to be opened up by 31 December 1990. For details see the volume by Dr Kevin Featherstone.

COM(88) 733 final: Proposal for a Council Directive on the application of Community rules on procedures for the award of public supply and public works contracts
Official Journal C15 19 January 1989, pp 8-9
The Commission has produced a revised proposal for enforcing the rules concerning supplies and works contracts awarded by national and local government

bodies. At present companies may be reluctant to take action against granting authorities because they fear negative repercussions in their relations with them. In case of emergency this proposal allows for the suspension of contract award procedures by the Commission and the right for it to intervene in national courts. It has encountered considerable opposition. In June 1989 the Council reached agreement on its 'common position'; the Commission has not obtained the right to intervene in national appeals bodies as it had wanted.

SMEs should note that the Commission is seeking fuller coverage of tender invitations in the 'S' series of the Official Journal and by the TED data bank.


## Freedom of Movement of Capital and Integration of Financial Services

Vol 9:  The 'Cost of Non-Europe' in Financial Services, Office for Official Publications of the EC, Luxembourg
This report by Price Waterhouse points out that the financial services market is large (6% of Community GDP), plays a substantial role in the development of other sectors, and is developing technically to a point at which the barriers of international borders seem irrelevant. The implications for SMEs are enormous as, with the creation of a European financial area, businesses will have greater opportunities to shop around for credit facilities, investment opportunities and insurance contracts to suit their needs. There will be greater variety of more competitive services on offer as a consequence of (a) the freedom of capital movement, (b) free trade within a unified European financial services market and (c) standardization of banking technology across Europe with a view to 'interoperability'. The most important aspect of Commission policy is the emphasis on deregulation of services so that market forces are likely to play a large role.


COM(87) 550 final:  Communication from the Commission:

Small and Medium Sized Enterprises

## Creation of a European financial area

This document builds on COM(83) 207 final and COM(86) 292 final and deals with the implementation of the liberalization of capital movements. In the Capital Movements Directive 88/361 agreement was reached. Already Britain, Denmark and West Germany have no exchange controls. The others, apart from Greece, Ireland, Portugal and Spain, must comply by July 1990; these four countries will have to open themselves up by the end of 1992 unless severe problems arise.

## COM(87) 715 final: 'The Second Banking Directive'

This proposal aims to create a truly internal market in banking, in which any credit institution authorized in a Member State will be able to establish branches and to offer its services freely throughout the EC to citizens and to businesses, from 1993, without further authorization (the concept of a 'Community passport'). It will still be subject to local business rules. At the same time the principle of mutual recognition of authorizations and supervisory systems must be founded on the prior harmonization of essential supervisory rules: hence the proposed Solvency Ratio Directive and an Own Funds Directive, COM(88) 194 and COM(86) 169 respectively.

## Second Council Directive of 22 June 1988 on the Co-ordination of Laws, Regulations and Administrative Provisions Relating to Direct Insurance, other then Life Insurance and Laying Down Provisions to Facilitate the Effective Exercise of freedom to provide services and amending Directive 73/239/EEC Council Directive 88/357/EEC. Official Journal L172, 4 July 1988, p.1.

When it takes effect in 1992, a genuine wholesale market in 'large risk' insurance will be allowed to develop. However, policy holders must be companies with more than 250 employees, or a turnover greater than 12.8 million ECUs or a balance sheet of over 6.2 million ECUs. Such companies are assumed to be better equipped to assess the financial viability of their insurer.

Small and Medium Sized Enterprises

This approach is being followed by planned action on life and car insurance. The Directive lays down special provisions relating to freedom to provide insurance services (other than life insurance) and objective standards of competence, experience and good repute. Where a Member State lays down any criteria for provision of services it must use those of the Directive and apply them equally to home and international companies.

COM(88) 778: Proposal for a Council Directive on investment services in the securities field
This proposal extends the concept of a 'Community passport', with one-country authorization, to cover securities and investment businesses.

**Promoting SMEs by Competition Policy Provisions**

COM(88) 232 final: Seventeenth report by the Commission on competition policy, 26 May 1988.
Articles 85 and 86 of the Treaty of Rome
Article 85(1) prohibits as 'incompatible with the Common Market' any agreements which prevent, restrict or distort competition within the EC (e.g. to share markets or sources of supply, to fix purchase or selling prices), whether between 'competitors' or between manufacturers and distributors or licensees. In 1986 the Commission extended its definition of agreements of minor importance which, in general, do not warrant an application of Article 85. The quantitative limits are set at a 5% market share of the firms involved and a combined annual turnover of 200 million ECUs i.e. not applying to SMEs. The level of fine imposed by the Commission is discretionary and depends on the duration and seriousness of the infringement; heavy fines are often imposed.
Article 86 ensures that companies do not abuse dominant market positions (e.g. the decision against Boosey and Hawkes in 1987). The Commission may simply require the abuse to be terminated or also impose a fine.

## Small and Medium Sized Enterprises

The competition rules can provide a valuable weapon in protecting the interests of SMEs against powerful competitors, suppliers or customers. SMEs suffering damages as a result of breaches of either Article 85 or Article 86 (e.g. refusal to supply products or the implementation of discriminatory trading conditions) may lodge complaints with the Commission at no cost. The Commission has extensive powers of investigation (Council Regulation 62/17) and can adopt decisions which are legally binding. Contact DG IV (Competition), Division Al General Competition Policy, 200 rue de la Loi, B-1049 Brussels. Also read 'EEC Competition Rules - Guide for SMEs', European Documentation 83/84, obtainable from the Commission's Information Offices.

Under Article 85(3) the Commission may exempt individual agreements from the prohibition of Article 85(1) where they improve the production or distribution of goods, promote technical or economic progress or allow consumers a fair share of the resulting benefits. In particular, block exemption regulations are of great importance to SMEs because no notification is required, thus avoiding time-consuming procedures. Several block exemption regulations are of direct relevance to SMEs either because of the nature of the activity or because of the conditions for application relating to market share and turnover. Examples are:

1. non-reciprocal exclusive distribution agreements between competitors are only allowed if at least one of the parties has an annual turnover of less than 100 million ECUs;
2. exclusive purchasing agreements (e.g. service stations and public houses); the regulation 1984/83 prevents the purchaser from being excessively bound to the supplier;
3. motor vehicle distribution and service agreements; the regulation 1985/123 ensures that car dealers are not made overly dependent on the supplier;
4. the patent licensing block exemption regulation 1984/2349 both allows small firms (as licensees) to gain access to new technologies and encourages the

innovative activities of small firms which (as licensors) can thus exploit their inventions throughout the EC via (bigger) licensees;

5. the block exemption of specialized agreements (1985/417), which applies only where market share (20%) and turnover thresholds (500 million ECUs) are not exceeded, was specifically created to allow SMEs to improve their production processes and thereby strengthen their competitive position;

6. the research and development block exemption regulation (1985/418) provides that competing companies which together have a market share of less than 20% may engage in joint research and development and joint exploitation of the results; this criterion covers in effect all such agreements involving SMEs and is important.

Of particular interest to SMEs are the block exemption regulations on know-how licensing and franchising agreements. In 1988 the Commission announced its intention of speeding up authorizations. See Regulation No 4087/88: Official Journal L359 1988, pp46-52. Through a series of test cases (Pronuptia, Yves Rocher and Computerland) the Commission has been developing its policy towards the system of franchising, which offers important possibilities for small firms.


## Promoting SMEs by Company Law and Tax Law Provisions

COM(88) 101 final: Proposal for a twelfth Council Directive on company law concerning single-member private limited companies

This proposal draws its inspiration both from the SME Action Programme and from the 1986 Action Programme on Employment Growth which underlined the need to encourage single-person businesses as a means of boosting selfemployment. Member States which seek to promote the access of individual entrepreneurs to the status of a company are Denmark (since 1973), West Germany (1980), France (1985), the Netherlands (1986) and Belgium (1987). Provisions for single-member companies do not exist in Britain, Greece, Ireland, Italy and Spain. Draft legislation has been before the Luxembourg Parliament since 1985, whilst Portugal introduced legislation for single-person businesses with limited liability in 1986. In Denmark, the Netherlands and West Germany such companies can be formed by artificial as well as natural persons. The aim of this proposed Directive is to harmonize this national legislation and extend limited liability protection for one-person businesses to other states. Its origin was the SME Task Force, and it is in effect a joint proposal with DG XV.

ECOSOC delivered a favourable opinion, suggesting that the proposal should contain a minimum capital requirement for the single-member company (because third parties were being exposed to risk). A favourable view was expected from the European Parliament. In the discussions at Council working group level criticisms were directed not so much at the principles behind the proposal as at details (e.g. Denmark and West Germany wanted to allow companies to be formed also by artificial persons; the Commission believed that this created a lack of transparency as chains of complex companies can be created in this way). On 14 June 1989 the Council of Ministers adopted a 'common position'; the Directive will have to be transposed into national legislation before 1 January 1992. The Directive does in fact embrace the wide range of provisions in national legislation, including anonymous single-person companies.


COM(88) 292 final: Proposal for a Council Directive amending Directive 78/660/EEC on annual accounts and Directive 83/349/EEC on consolidated accounts with respect to the exemptions for small and medium sized companies and to the drawing up and publication of accounts in ECU
This proposal aims to harmonize and simplify the accounting requirements placed on SMEs by amending the Fourth Company Law Directive (78/660). The 1978 Directive laid down common rules for the drawing up, publication and auditing of the annual accounts and

annual reports of limited liability companies. It also offered Member States <u>the option</u> of granting exemptions for small and medium sized companies with respect to the content and form of the accounts, publication of the annual accounts and annual report, and auditing. Three thresholds for the definition of such companies were selected: balance sheet total, net turnover, and number of employees (the two financial thresholds were later raised by a Council Directive of 27 November 1984).

1. Small companies have a balance sheet total of up to 1,550,000 ECUs, a net turnover of up to 3,200,000 ECUs and an average number of employees of up to 50. They may be allowed to draw up only an abridged balance sheet and profit and loss account and abridged notes on the accounts; to publish only an abridged balance sheet and abridged notes; not to publish the profit and loss account, annual report and auditors' report; and not to have their accounts audited.

2. Medium-sized companies have a balance sheet total of up to 6,200,000 ECUs, a net turnover of up to 12,800,000 ECUs and an average number of employees up to 250. They may be allowed to draw up only an abridged profit and loss account; and to publish only an abridged balance sheet and profit and loss account and abridged notes.

In practice Member States have varied in the extent to which they have taken advantage of this option (tending to adopt it more for small than for medium-sized companies). This new proposal sought to reinforce the objective of establishing similar requirements for companies throughout the EC and to apply the spirit of the SME Action Programme by making the exemptions compulsory for small companies. The proposal also introduces a certain flexibility for the two financial thresholds, whilst for the definition of small companies Member States may descend to a minimum of twenty-five. In this way more liberal states are to be allowed to extend simplification of requirements. Additionally, under certain conditions SMEs may keep their accounting documents available to the public at the registered office of the company (as in West Germany) instead of having to file them with a register as provided for by the First Company Law Directive (68/151). This provision meets the concern of SMEs for confidentiality whilst preserving the basic principle of the Fourth Directive i.e. that all limited liability companies must publish accounts and that these accounts must be available without restrictions to any interested party. Finally, the proposal will make it possible for companies operating in several EC countries to draw up and publish their accounts in ECUs if they so wish. This provision serves the Commission's policy of increasing European monetary integration.

The political context of the proposed Directive was delicate. Pressure for change came from the SME Task Force which had drawn on the advice of business consultants, advisers and various European associations representing SMEs; and from SMEs in West Germany where the implementation of the Fourth Directive had been delayed till 1988 and the new requirements especially on publicity were seen as onerous. Resistance came internally from DG XV which had drawn up the Fourth Directive and was already frustrated by slow implementation.

The ECOSOC opinion of March 1989 was very negative. It took a stricter view on accounting requirements for small firms in the interest of greater protection of third persons and consequently opposed the idea of compulsory exemptions for small firms. By contrast, the Legal Affairs Committee of the European Parliament was much more favourable to the whole approach; its amendments focused on the flexibility of the financial thresholds and the option of publicity at the registered office. Within the Council of Ministers this proposal was pushed strongly by the Spanish Presidency (which was especially keen on SMEs) and enthusiastically backed by West Germany. Overall, however, the proposal was more politically difficult then COM(88) 101 final.

Small and Medium Sized Enterprises

<u>COM(84) 727 final: Proposal for a tenth Directive of</u>
<u>the council based on articles 54(3) of the Treaty</u>
<u>concerning cross-border mergers of public limited</u>
<u>companies</u>
   This proposal aims to facilitate cross-border mergers
of public limited companies within the EC by simplifying
procedures for creating or restructuring enterprises.
At the moment the legislation of certain Member States
either does not allow or does not provide for such
mergers and other Member States subject such operations
to prohibitive conditions (e.g. the unanimous approval
of the shareholders of the company being acquired).
Complex and unwieldly techniques have been evolved to
cope with mergers involving companies which are governed
by the laws of different Member States, and the proposal
aims to simplify the procedures. At the same time the
proposal argues that certain rules need to be harmonized
more stringently than is the case for national mergers
particularly to ensure that third parties (e.g.
creditors) and employees are better informed (the
contents of the draft terms of merger, the protection of
creditors of acquired companies, the date on which the
merger takes effect, the causes of nullity of a merger).
Overall, progress on the proposal remains slow.


<u>Council Regulation No 85/2137 on the European economic</u>
<u>interest grouping (EEIG)</u>
   This new, but limited initiative to promote cross-
frontier business co-operation was adopted by the
Council of Ministers on 25 July 1985 and took effect on
1 July 1989. It is the first successful attempt at an
EC instrument in the field of corporate law. Formulated
by DG XV, the publicity campaign in 1989 involves co-
operation with DG XXIII to stress that the EEIG is
specially designed for SMEs and that co-operation
amongst SMEs is their best strategy for success in the
Single European Market. The aim of the EEIG mechanism
is to avoid formalities (e.g. associated with the
creation and liquidation of companies) by providing a
very flexible instrument of co-operation, somewhere
between a contract and a company, in carrying out

78

specific projects (e.g. for a limited three-month period or to respond to a call for tender for a public works contract). It can also serve as a progressive instrument, beginning with limited co-operation and perhaps even developing in the long term to create a company. The EEIG is designed not to affect the economic and legal independence of a participating company.

SMEs might find the EEIG useful for the following types of joint activity: provision of specialized legal services or accountancy or management consultancy services; research and development; purchasing, production and selling (e.g. advanced consumer electronics, quality control of substances, maintenance, computerized data processing, and the formation of multidisciplinary consortia in the construction industry to tender for public or private contracts). The more 'high quality' and professional SMEs are likely to be attracted to use it, particularly in the context of EC research programmes. SMEs should also note that an EEIG constituted in one Member State can operate throughout the EC (even in Member States which have not yet adapted their national legislation).

The EEIG proposal was French-inspired. France already has this type of instrument within its national company law. Other states indicating a substantial interest in the EEIG are Belgium and Italy.

Business advisers are worried about how the EEIG will work for tax purposes, not least because the implementation measures have to be taken at national level (e.g. on registration procedures and the taxes to be applied) and the Council Regulation speaks only of the principle of tax transparency. Profits will be divided up between the parties according to the contract creating the EEIG and taxed as part of the profits of the individual parties.


## COM(88) 320 final: Statute for the European company

Despite failed efforts since the initial proposal of 1970, a new impetus was given to debate about the concept of a European company statute in June 1988 by a memorandum from the Commission. A formal proposal on this subject was seen as essential to the completion of the Single European Market. Under this new memorandum the European company statute would coexist with national systems of company law and would be entirely optional: it would be available for those seeking cross-frontier mergers. Member States could also choose between several formulae on worker participation. Worker participation remains the most difficult issue. Details are to be found in the volume by Dr Kevin Featherstone. In early 1989 the proposal was being drafted. Of importance to SMEs is the question of the threshold from which worker participation in management would be compulsory. It was expected that a threshold of 500 workers would be established; below this figure there would be no form of compulsory worker participation.

COM(88) 823 final: Proposal for a thirteenth Council Directive on company law concerning takeover and other general bids Official Journal 14 March 1989, 89/C64/08.
The SME Task-Force was successful in securing amendments to this proposal in order to reduce the administrative formalities for SMEs and to confine its application to public companies, limited by shares, only (as was the case with Member State legislation). See Article 5 'Exemptions on the Basis of Size of the Offeree Company' which waives the obligation to make a bid (in the interests of equality of treatment) on persons wishing to attain a certain level of participation in a company (maximum of 33 1/3%).

Proposal for a Council Regulation on the control of concentrations between undertakings (merger control regulation) Official Journal C92, 31st October 1973. Various amended proposals (eg. 1981)
This proposal is based on Article 149 of the EC Treaty and aims to give the European Commission powers to control mergers 'with a Community dimension'. In April 1989 the proposal was revised to change the threshold for mergers coming under EC scrutiny from 1

billion ECUs to 5 billion ECUs at first, falling to 2
billion ECUs at the end of 1992. Informally the Commission indicated that this Regulation includes in itself
the application of Articles 85 and 86 of the EC Treaty.
On the other hand, the Commission undertakes never to
invoke Articles 85 and 86 for mergers whose thresholds
are lower than 2 billion ECUs (after 1992) or 5 billion
ECUs.

COM(86) 444 final: Proposal for a Council Directive
amending Directive 77/388/EEC on the harmonization of
the laws of the Member States relating to turnover taxes
in respect of the common value-added tax scheme
applicable to small and medium sized businesses.
COM(87) 321/2 rev. final: Proposal for a Council
Directive completing the common system of VAT and
amending Directive 77/388/EEC - Approximation of VAT
rates.
This proposal seeks to improve and simplify the Sixth
VAT Directive which laid down rules on the basis of
assessment for VAT in the Member States and on
exemptions and graduated VAT relief. The Sixth
Directive gave Member States a large degree of freedom
to introduce exemption schemes up to a low threshold of
5,000 ECUs. As a consequence, some Member States had no
exemption limits; others based exemption on turnover
(e.g. Britain whose threshold infringed EC law); whilst
others based exemptions on tax payable.
In order to harmonize and simplify VAT arrangements
for SMEs, the Commission proposed a **compulsory** exemption
scheme at the higher level of 10,000 ECUs, applied to
turnover only, and an **optional** top exemption limit of
35,000 ECUs (effectively legalizing the situation in
Britain). It also proposed a common simplified
accounting scheme for SMEs with an annual turnover of
less than 200,000 ECUs. In particular, the proposal
backed the principle of payment on cash received. Under
the present system VAT is due once a company has
invoiced somebody for goods, even though the goods may
be paid for six months later or not at all. To overcome
this cash-flow problem, SMEs were to owe VAT only when

they were paid for goods. Further elements of simplification included harmonization of the timing of VAT returns and returns for direct taxation (i.e. annual, with provisional advanced payments being provided during the course of the year) and the opportunity for Member States to introduce flat-rate percentages for calculating deductible VAT as a proportion of turnover (with Commission approval). In short, Member States were to be given a good deal of freedom to simplify VAT arrangements for SMEs.

This proposal was blocked in the Council of Ministers. Several members, especially the southern states, feared that they would lose a considerable amount of VAT revenue; others preferred to increase the optional element in the proposal (which made it useless to the Commission); and the Netherlands wanted to retain its very different concept of VAT arrangements for SMEs, emphasizing tax reduction rather than simplification. The contact is DG XXI/C/Customs Union and Indirect Taxation, rue d'Arlon 80, B-1040 Brussels.

## Proposal (at drafting stage in the Commission in early 1989) to harmonize the basis of assessment of taxes on the profits of enterprises

This proposal, which has been pending since 1985, has been the responsibility of DG XV, with the SME Task-Force seeking to have a significant impact on behalf of SMEs. The aim is to harmonize by laying down common rules of calculation of taxes on profits in order to both prevent distortion of competition and encourage SMEs. This issue is likely to loom large in the future. The proposal is likely to have the following basic elements:

1. the basic idea is to allow individual smaller companies to be taxed on the same basis as the rate for physical persons and to give them the option to be taxed at the corporate rate, thereby encouraging investment as profits are allocated to corporate uses;
2. the profits of companies are to be taxed at a

progressive rate; the smaller the profits, the lower the tax;

3. tax reform is to make easier the transmission of SMEs, which tend to disappear with the death of the owner or are bought by larger companies because of high inheritance and other taxes, by dissociating the fiscal regime from the distinction between company assets and the private assets of the owner;

4. the mere fact of changing the legal form of a company should not produce tax problems;

5. the need to lighten the taxation of revenue from licensing of patents and know how by innovatory SMEs that cannot exploit their own ideas but need to be encouraged.

COM(84) 404 final and (85) 319 final:  Harmonization of Member States' laws relating to tax arrangements for carry over of losses of undertakings
This proposal permits the carrying over of losses for tax purposes and is of value to SMEs in helping to improve their self-financing capacity and cash flows.

COM(76) 611 final:  Proposal for a Council Directive on the elimination of double taxation in connection with the adjustment of transfers of profits between associated enterprises (arbitration procedure)
This proposal aims to establish an arbitration procedure to eliminate double taxation affecting associated firms which operate on a cross-frontier basis.  The proposal is especially valuable to SMEs because double taxation affects them more severely than large companies with greater financial assets.

**Health and Safety at Work**

COM(87) 520 final:  Communication from the Commission on its programme concerning safety, hygiene and health at work.  Council Resolution 88/C28/01 of 21 December 1987 Proposal for a Council Directive on the introduction of

<u>measures to encourage improvements in the health and safety of workers at the workplace</u> Official Journal 30 May 1988, 88/C141/01

Under the EC Treaty (Articles 117 and 118) the Commission has implemented two Action Programmes on safety and health at work since 1978. These programmes were the subject of two Council Resolutions (29 June 1978 and 27 February 1984). In this context ten Directives (seven adopted by May 1988) were drafted on the protection of workers exposed to physical and chemical agents at work and the prevention of major accident hazards related to chemicals. On the basis of the new provisions of the Single European Act (Article 118A (1) on the harmonization of improvements in the conditions of protection of the health and safety of workers and Article 118B which stresses the need to promote the dialogue between the two sides of industry) the Commission decided to draw up a new work programme. The new programme was outlined in COM(87) 520 final and covers five subjects: safety and ergonomics (especially the high-risk sectors of construction, agriculture and work at sea); occupational health and hygiene; information; training; social dialogue; and SMEs. With reference to Article 118A of the Single European Act, which recognizes the special needs of SMEs in this area, the Commission intends to ensure that Directives do not impose undue administrative, financial and legal constraints on SMEs, to review existing regulations and their application to SMEs, to improve the information and advice available to SMEs and to prepare training modules. Similarly, the proposed Council Directive (see above) provides that the application of its provisions may be 'modulated' to take account of the size of the enterprise and 'socio-economic factors'. In this context five other draft Directives were submitted to the Council in February 1988 covering workplaces; work equipment; personal protective equipment; work with visual display units; and handling of heavy loads involving risk of back injury. In April 1989 the Council adopted its 'common positions' on the first three of these Directives; their application is planned for the end of 1992.

Small and Medium Sized Enterprises

## Promoting SMEs in EC Employment, Training and Youth Policies

The European Social Fund
<u>Commission Decision of 4 May 1988 on the guidelines for the management of the European Social Fund in the financial years 1989 to 1991</u>.   Official Journal 88/319/EEC
    The ESF aims to increase employment opportunities in the EC by providing financial assistance (normally providing the same percentage level as public authorities) for training and retraining schemes and the resettlement of workers moving from one occupation or area to another.   Finance goes to projects receiving public support but can apply to private as well as public projects provided these create or retain jobs. Under the 1983 Fund Regulation (amended 1985) emphasis was on young people and the long-term unemployed in the EC's absolute priority regions; this emphasis was confirmed in the new Fund Regulation of 1989.   SMEs should note that the ESF can be a valuable source of temporary supplementary funding for vocational training and retraining projects and can support (up to three years) innovatory projects with a European dimension or which form part of integrated development programmes. For details see the volume by Margareta Holmstedt. Contact: DG V (Employment, Social Affairs), 200 rue de la Loi, B-1049 Brussels, and the relevant national government department.


<u>Council Resolution of 7 June 1984 concerning the contribution of local employment initiatives in combating unemployment</u> (Official Journal No C161 of 21 June 1984)
    This Resolution asks Member States to adopt political guidelines for the promotion of local employment initiatives and calls upon the Commission to implement Community action in the form of aid from the ESF, advisory and information transfer programmes and specific studies.   In the earlier Communication from the Commission to the Council, COM(83) 662 final, <u>Community</u>

Small and Medium Sized Enterprises

<u>Action to Combat Unemployment - Contribution of Local Employment Initiatives</u>, LEIs had been defined as: 'those initiatives which have occurred at the local level - often involving co-operation between individuals, action groups, social partners and local and regional authorities - with the specific aim of providing additional, permanent employment opportunities through the creation of new small-scale enterprises'. It points out that LEIs resemble in many respects other traditional SMEs but tend to be distinguishable from them through the reasons for their creation, the social context of those involved and the sectors in which they are active. The term LEI seems to embrace conventional businesses, co-operatives and community businesses that operate on the basis of small-scale local community involvement, assisted by an 'animateur' or local development agent (whether local authorities, enterprise boards or trusts, co-operative development agencies, churches or trade unions). They represent social as well as economic innovations, dedicated to the objective of 'worthwhile' employment and responding to gaps in the market place, and often set up by people excluded from the declining traditional sectors - women, young people, immigrant workers, older people or the long-term unemployed.

DG V has focused its attention on developing support activities for local development agencies as follows:

1. The establishment of ELISE, the European Information Exchange Network on Local Employment Initiatives, in 1985. Its aims were: to make information available to all private and public bodies and individuals active in local development; to organize the sharing of experiences amongst regions and countries; and to link a minimum of 300 organizations by the network. At the heart of the documentation and information service of ELISE was a data base embracing four areas: local and regional development; enterprise and SMEs; training at local and regional levels; and social integration of disadvantaged groups. The data base embraced the organizations and innovative experiences in the four areas, encouraged information

networking amongst member organizations and assisted the production of a monthly newsletter and the provision of a weekly information service for members only. ELISE's development clarified the EC's role as essentially technical i.e. data base development and encouragement of networking. Over time ELISE became more distant from DG V, working more closely with other directorates-general notably DG XVI. It also became more dependent on its members for revenue after 1 January 1989. Contact: ELISE/A.E.I.D.L., 34 rue Breydel, B-1040 Brussels, tel: (2) 230 52 34. Note also ELISE's (first) European Directory of Local Development Agencies, 1989, with details of almost 1700 agencies covering all Member States.

2. Since 1986 an annual exchange programme between local development agents in the twelve Member States. Over sixty agents each year, mostly from local authorities, have been involved in seven- to ten-day visits on such subjects as training and marketing strategy and, in 1989, on '1992' issues. The visits are seen as a catalyst for energy and motivation and a means of enhancing the credibility and recognition of such agents and LEIs. As in the case of ELISE, DG V collaborated closely with EGLEI, the European Group for Local Employment Initiatives. See 'Broadening the Horizons of Enterprise', ELISE 1987.

3. In 1986 DG V launched the Research and Action Programme on the Local Development of the Employment Market, a study of twelve exemplary pilot projects in twelve different regions of the EC, organized by Haris Martinos. The study underlined the value of the local approach to expansion of SMEs, technology transfer, training young people and helping the long-term unemployed. It suggested greater technical assistance from the EC and greater responsiveness to local needs in the operation of the EC structural funds. Published 1988 as 'Twelve European Regions under the Microscope', European Service Network, Brussels.

Small and Medium Sized Enterprises

COM(86) 784 final:  Follow-up to the Council Resolution
of 7 June 1984.  Communication from the Commission
Resolution on the communication from the Commission to
the Council
COM(86) 784 final concerning the contribution of LEIs in
combating unemployment. Official Journal No C156 of 15
June 1987
   COM(86) 784 final reported progress on achievements
at the level of Member States and proposed priority
actions to improve the environment of LEIs.  The French
government had been the first to introduce a national
programme of subsidy to LEIs in 1982.  Community
business is especially strong in Ireland; whilst in
Britain, Business in the Community, an association of
major companies, has been particularly involved in the
development of local enterprise agencies to support
local small and start-up businesses, and large companies
like British Steel, British Coal, BAT Industries and
Rank-Xerox have supported new local initiatives in areas
adversely affected by their commercial decisions.  A
more general development is new partnerships between
large and small companies involving start-up packages,
spin-offs and management buy-outs, sub-contracting,
workshop provision, favourable finance, and research and
development and technology transfer.
   The Council Resolution encourages the Commission and
Member States to support LEIs, notably by removing
obstacles to their development and granting easier
access to financial instruments.


Council Resolution of 22 December 1986 on an action
programme for employment growth. Official Journal No
C340 of 31 December 1986.
   This Resolution outlines measures to promote the
creation of new businesses, including the development of
LEIs, with a view to improving the efficiency of labour
markets, training and activities to help the long-term
unemployed.


SEC(88) 1860 final:  Preparing small and medium sized

enterprises for Europe 1992:    Experimental training
schemes.  17 January 1989
     The aim of this experimental scheme is to test, in
conjunction with training and advisory agencies at the
sectoral or regional levels, a form of training to help
SME managers to develop a strategy for expansion in the
Single European Market.    This first dedicated SME
training programme was developed principally by the SME
Task-Force, DG III and DG V, building on a concept of
training worked out by CEDEFOP which is also preparing a
guide to training for SMEs.    It was clear that there
were plenty of general management training schemes
available; the problem was not supply, but how to
stimulate demand.    SMEs were reluctant to become
involved in such schemes because of issues of distance,
scarcity of time and doubts about relevance.    At the
same time management skills were a key determinant of
SME success.  Hence the scheme starts with the first key
step - the need to convince the heads of SMEs of the
importance of training.  The lever employed is the need
of SMEs to know what the Single European Market means
for them, particularly new competitive pressures.   The
demand for concrete information about '1992' is to be
used to stimulate an appetite for training.
     This scheme builds on existing sectoral and regional
training agents with experience of small businesses and
has two main dimensions:

1. After a call for proposals the Commission will select
   agents who will be provided with a training programme
   of six modules and supporting documents focusing on
   the elements of strategic management for '1992'.

2. The Commission will support regional or sectoral
   analyses preparatory to education and information
   seminars for SMEs on '1992' (see Official Journal No
   S27/57 of 9th February 1989).

     Later measures include: networking of training
projects and co-operation between training agencies;
training SME managers in co-operation strategies; and
promoting the role of large firms and banks in the

provision of training for SME managers. Co-ordination with the Business and Innovation Centres (DG XVI) is also under consideration to stress support for 'less-favoured' regions of the EC.


COMETT (Programme of the Community in education and training for technology). Council Decision in Official Journal No L222 on 8 August 1986.
COM(88) 36 final: The COMETT programme: A report of activities in 1987
Council Decision of 16 December 1988 adopting COMETT II (1990-1994). Official Journal 89/27/EEC
     COMETT aims to promote a **European dimension** in, and better co-operation between universities and industry related to **advanced training** for technologies; to adapt the content of training to technological and social change; and to improve training opportunities at local, regional and national levels. Projects will be favoured if they group together SMEs, larger companies and universities and involve new training initiatives. The first four-year phase covered the period 1986-9 inclusive; the second phase (1990-4) has an estimated budget of 200 million ECUs. First priority was given to the establishment of a European network of university/ enterprise training partnership (UETPs) as the infrastructure for the other activities supported, in particular an EC programme of transnational university /industry exchanges and EC-level joint training projects in conjunction with high-technology firms in fields where there is a shortage of trained staff. For guidance contact: COMETT Technical Assistance Unit, Avenue de Cortenberg 71, B-1040 Brussels, tel: (02) 733 97 55 and the national members of the EC's COMETT Committee in the relevant ministry: also the Task-Force for Human Resources, Education, Training and Youth in the Commission.


DELTA (Developing European learning through technological advance).
Pilot Phase - Proposal for a Council Regulation COM(87)

Small and Medium Sized Enterprises

<u>353 final.</u>
<u>Council Decision of 29 June 1988</u>. Official Journal
88/417/EEC.
The DELTA programme aims to focus the research and
development effort of EC industry, universities and
publishers on advanced techniques and infrastructures
required to support **distance open learning**. Projects
must be pre-competitive, cross-national, involve a
commercial enterprise and be concerned with advanced
educational and multi-media training through new
technologies (e.g. satellite transmission). There is an
important market here for SMEs. SMES can also benefit
from new opportunities for training and professional
updating. The pilot phase was to be followed by a five-
year main programme from 1989/90. Contact: DG XIII
(Telecommunications, Information Industries and
Innovation), 200 rue de la Loi, B-1049 Brussels, tel:
(02) 236 03 79.


<u>COM(85) 167 final: EUROTECNET (Community action</u>
<u>programme in the field of vocational training and new</u>
<u>information technologies)</u>
EUROTECNET aims to exchange information and
experience by developing a European **network** of
demonstration projects (some 135 in 1988), identified by
Member States for their model value as innovative
**vocational training** approaches; a programme of co-
ordinated **inter-project visits**; a series of **concerted
studies** on specific aspects of vocational training
linked to new technologies; **dissemination conferences;
specialized working parties; publications** (including a
newsletter three times a year); and **a data base**. The
purpose is to improve innovative projects in vocational
training for skilled workers by networking, and SMEs are
one of the four key target groups (the others are young
people with low qualifications, older skilled workers
and women). In 1989 a report on the 1985-8 programme is
due and will stress EUROTECNET'S catalytic function in
creating a reservoir of expert knowledge. The second
programme, which is being developed in 1989, is likely
to identify a more active role in disseminating good

practice, notably training materials and methodologies, and to stress that training is crucial for SMEs and must be adapted to specific industrial, educational and cultural conditions. Particularly notable has been the development of consortia of SMEs for training in new technologies (e.g. Turin in Italy) and the importance of local and regional governmental stimulus and action in France, Italy and West Germany. In the Netherlands a major venture capital bank has developed a training programme for SMEs; in France the pump manufacturing sector (strongly SME-based) has developed a concerted approach. See the brochure on Training for New Information Technologies and SMEs: EUROTECNET, European Centre for Work and Society, 1988. Contact: Task-Force for Human Resources, Education, Training and Youth. On the technical aspects contact: the European Centre for Work and Society, PO Box 3073, Hoogbrugstraat 43, NL-6202 NB Maastricht, tel: (043) 21 67 24.

COM(88) 841 final: Proposal for a Council Decision establishing the LINGUA programme to promote training in foreign languages in the EC. Proposal for a Council Decision for the promotion of the teaching and learning of foreign languages in the EC as part of the LINGUA programme.
The LINGUA programme aims at a quantitative and qualitative improvement in the teaching and learning of all the official languages of the EC, with particular emphasis on vocational training, improved communication skills and educational exchanges and on in-service training and preparation of foreign language teachers and trainers for this purpose. A first phase of five years (1990-4) is proposed, with full-scale operation beginning in 1991/2. SMEs in particular should note that the EC will provide support for:

1. the development of dissemination of 'foreign language 1992 audits', designed particularly for SMEs, to specify the extent of their foreign languages needs and training requirements and to be followed by developmental activities involving a 'reasonable

sample' of companies;

2. the development (on a pilot basis) of specific foreign language training materials for different economic sectors (e.g. the legal sector) in the various EC languages: and priority will be given to sectors in which SMEs are strongly represented and the impact of the Single European Market is likely to be greatest;

3. projects demonstrating the potential of open learning methods for foreign language teaching (e.g. satellite).

The British government objected strongly to this proposal, based in part on the cost of the programme and in part on the principle of interference in national education policy. In May 1989 the Council approved the LINGUA programme, allocating slightly less than originally envisaged, for 'young people undergoing professional, vocational and technical education'. Member States were left to define what vocational education meant and whether or not it should be extended to schools. On the subject of vocational training, the LINGUA programme says that it is 'up to each of the Member States to define this and to narrow the scope or to widen it to, for instance, all above 16 years or all in post-compulsory education'.

The Young Worker Exchange Programme:    Third joint programme (1985-90 inclusive). Official Journal L331 19 December 1984.

This programme aims to give young people (18-28 years) an opportunity to live and work in another EC country in order to develop their vocational knowledge and experience, their knowledge of living and working in the host country and their knowledge of the EC. Young workers must be employed or available on the labour market and have received basic vocational training or practical work experience. Up to 4,000 young people are now helped annually on short-term exchanges (3 weeks - 3 months) or long-term exchanges (4-16 months), mostly in the service sector. SMEs should note the opportunity offered by this programme and the key role played by the national independent promoting body which should be contacted.

Council Decision of 1 December 1987:    PETRA (The European Community action programme for the vocational training of young people and their preparation for adult and working life).  Official Journal L346 10 December 1987, 87/569/EEC.

This programme aims to support and supplement the efforts of Member States to ensure that all young people who so wish receive one year's, or, if possible, two or more years', vocational training after the completion of their full-time compulsory education.  The purpose is to raise the standard of vocational training and ensure that it leads to recognized qualifications; to diversify the range of training available; and to assist the adaptation of vocational training to technological, economic and social change.

PETRA is not specifically designed for SMEs, but SMEs should note two parts of the Action Programme through which they could benefit.

1. The European Network of Training Initiatives seeks to give a European dimension to training measures at national, regional and local levels by facilitating transnational, co-operative partnerships based on innovative projects.  Thus the Commission will circulate a 'catalogue' of project profiles, provide study visit and partnership grants and arrange workshops e.g. for the twinning of mini-enterprises or youth co-operatives aimed at joint production and marketing.  New types of training consortia are being encouraged, including co-operation between small firms and (vocational) schools and colleges to create new opportunities for fully-fledged training programmes or apprenticeships.  Stress is also being placed on opening up new opportunities for non-traditional training providers like co-operatives and 'self-managed' firms.  In addition, mini-enterprises and youth co-operatives are being encouraged to

develop transnational contacts in enterprise
education schemes e.g. on joint projects, staff
exchange and use of new communication technology.
Also of interest is the theme of creating new forms
of training in new non-agricultural occupations in
rural areas: e.g. tourism, cultural heritage, ecology
and environment.

2. Youth Initiative Projects gives small grants, for one
year, to projects planned, organized and managed by
young people themselves, in such areas as training,
youth information and the development of employment
opportunities, many of them involving disadvantaged
young people. These projects are intended to sharpen
policy makers' awareness of the needs and aspirations
of young people and to provide suggestions for how
training can be made more accessible to young people.
Youth co-operatives and workshops have been strongly
represented. Contact: PETRA Support Unit, IFAPLAN,
Square Ambiorix 32, B-1040 Brussels, tel: (02) 230 71
06.


Council Recommendation of 13 December 1984 on the
promotion of positive action for women 86/635/EEC
Equal opportunities for women: Medium-term Community
programme 1986-1990. Council Resolution of 24 July 1986
Official Journal 88/C75/02 invitation to tender for the
management of the scheme of grant aid for the creation
by women of small businesses or local employment
initiatives
The European Commission's aid programme for women was
extended in 1988 to women wishing to set up their own
business. Start-up aid is granted for the first year of
activity, provided that the business creates jobs for
women. Subsidies rise to a maximum of 5,000 ECUs,
taking the form of 1,000 ECUs per full-time job created
(or the equivalent in part-time jobs). They will be
granted as a priority to businesses providing jobs for
underprivileged groups of women (migrant women, women
going back to work after several years without a job
etc.) or operating in sectors where women are poorly

represented.  Commission aid can be important in winning credibility for projects at the national level, with aid in 1988 being granted to 128 women's businesses in a range of different sectors.  Projects also benefit from the support of the Commission's network of experts on local employment initiatives for women, circulating information in their own countries and advising project promoters on how to obtain access to aid.

Contact: Women's Bureau, DG V/A/4, and read the project profiles 'Women in Business', published by ELISE.  See also the volume in this series by Margareta Holmstedt.


**Promoting SMEs in EC Regional Policy**

<u>Council Regulation No 4253/88 of 19 December 1988 laying down provisions for implementing Regulation No 2052/88 as regards co-ordination of the activities of the different structural funds between themselves and with the operations of the European Investment Bank and the other existing financial instruments</u>
<u>Council Regulation No 4254/88 of 19 December 1988 laying down provisions for implementing Regulation No 2052/88 as regards the European Regional Development Fund</u>
The context of these two Regulations is provided by Council Regulation No 2052/88 of 24 June 1988 on the tasks of the Structural Funds (the European Regional Development Fund, the European Social Fund and the European Agricultural Guidance and Guarantee Fund - Guidance Section) and their effectiveness and co-ordination; by the agreement of the European Council on 11-12 February 1988 to double in real terms commitment appropriations for the Structural Funds by 1993; and by the emphasis in the Single European Act on 'strengthening economic and social cohesion', particularly by reducing disparities between the various regions and the backwardness of the least-favoured regions.  For details see the volume by Copperthwaite and Mellors.

'Complementarity' and 'partnership' are defined as central policy principles and find expression in the provisions for three-to-five year Community support frameworks establishing joint priorities and forms of assistance for each Member State and for a renewed emphasis on integrated approaches by the Structural Funds (Articles 8 and 13 respectively of Regulation 4253/88).

SMEs should note in particular Regulation 4254/88: Article 1(c) the development of indigenous potential in the regions by measures which encourage and support local development initiatives and the activities of SMEs (especially assistance to business services, technology transfer, improved access to capital, investment aid and the provision of small-scale infrastructure); and Article 6 (Global Grants) by which the Commission may entrust to appropriate intermediaries, including regional development organizations, designated by the Member State in agreement with the Commission, the management of global grants, which it shall use primarily to assist local development initiatives. Those provisions effectively develop Article 15 of the old Regulation 1787/84 to make development of indigenous potential a key theme of the new Regulation. They also complement the SME Task-Force's new emphasis on 'seed capital' provision and the EIB's global loan mechanism. SMEs can approach regional and local authorities, chambers of commerce and trade associations and ask them to take the initiative in developing assistance measures for SMEs.

Community Programmes: Council Regulation No 3300/86: The STAR programme (advanced telecommunications services); Council Regulation No 3301/86: The VALOREN programme (Exploitation of indigenous energy potential); Council Regulation No 328/88: The RESIDER programme (conversion of steel areas);
Council Regulation No 2506/88: The RENAVAL programme (conversion of shipbuilding areas)

These multiannual programmes, undertaken on the Commission's initiative, had their basis in Article 7 of the old Regulation 1787/84 and represent priorities in the management of ERDF resources. In Greece and Spain

Small and Medium Sized Enterprises

notably approved STAR and VALOREN assistance programmes have targeted help on SMEs (e.g. for greater energy efficiency). Articles 2 of the RENAVAL and RESIDER programmes specifically mention support for the growth of SMEs, for new activities and for innovation as well as for infrastructural measures. Also, co-operatives, the self-employed and other businesses are eligible for Fund assistance. SMEs should contact the relevant ministry for information about programmes and how to become involved in project tender procedures or how to benefit from new services.

National Programmes of Community Interest (NPCIs)

NPCIs have developed alongside Community programmes but differ in being undertaken on the initiative of Member States and adopted in agreement with the Commission. They may be independent programmes or the ERDF component of Integrated Development Operations (IDOs) or of Integrated Mediterranean Programmes (IMPs). After three years of the old Regulation the EC had adopted forty-eight NPCIs, with twenty-three in France and nine in Britain. Encouragement of SMEs was a general feature of these NPCIs. For details see Thirteenth Annual Report (1987) of the ERDF, COM(88) 728 final.

Specific Community Measures

These measures are undertaken on the Commission's initiative, were first introduced in 1980 and were extended in Article 45 of the Regulation 1787/84. Some run till 1989 and some till 1991. They constituted the first use of the programme approach and have focused on aid schemes for SMEs and for infrastructural investment to exploit the indigenous development potential particularly of areas adversely affected by sectoral problems (e.g. steel, shipbuilding, textile and fishery areas) and border areas (Ireland/Northern Ireland). Another twenty-four new special programmes were approved

Small and Medium Sized Enterprises

in 1987.

**Promoting SMEs in EC Rural Development Policy**

<u>Council Regulation 77/335 direct assistance from the
European Agricultural Guidance and Guarantee Fund
(EAGGF)</u>

This programme aims to support schemes or individual
projects relating to the processing or marketing of
agricultural products, and the choice of product and
project priorities is revised and updated regularly by
DG VI (Agriculture). Projects involve assistance for
new equipment and new processing techniques and for
investment in energy saving; must form part of specific
national programmes approved by the EC; must involve
sectors or regions where there is no over-capacity; must
provide long-term economic benefits to producers and
agricultural production; concern processing or marketing
of conventional agricultural products; and, preferably,
require two-to-three years of support. Most
beneficiaries are SMEs. The EAGGF Guidance Section will
benefit from the doubling of the Structural Funds
(agreed February 1988) and is affected by Council
Regulation No 2052/88 (see the section on EC regional
policy).

<u>Council Regulation 86/4028 Community measures to improve
and adapt structures in the fisheries and aquaculture
sectors</u>

Projects must fall within the framework of specific
multiannual guidance programmes approved by the
Commission and be submitted to the Commission through
the relevant national ministry. The nature of the
projects (e.g. modernization of the fishing fleet, port
facilities) meant that opportunities for SMEs are
limited. Contact: DG XIV (Fisheries).

<u>COM(88) 501 final: The future of rural society</u>

This Communication from the Commission reflects the

fact that rural development has been chosen as one of the priority objectives for the reformed Structural Funds (see Council Regulation No 2052/88). It seeks to outline a Community approach to the problems of rural society, guided by the three themes of economic and social cohesion, unavoidable restructuring of agriculture and protection of the environment. In relationship to two of the three types of problem area (areas of rural decline and very marginal areas) the emphasis is on mobilizing the indigenous development potential. Areas of rural decline require integrated rural development programmes that stress economic diversification through promotion of SMEs and vocational training; whilst very marginal areas need to strengthen one-person and very small businesses. The particular problems of SMEs in these areas are identified as relative economic isolation and ageing production methods, and particular emphasis is placed on improving services and service industries (e.g. business service centres, telecommunications, amenities, training) and on promoting rural tourism. The new EAGGF Regulation reflects these priorities, which are complemented in the priorities of the proposed NCI V. SMEs should be encouraging local and regional authorities and trade associations to take advantage of the new opportunities.


## Promoting SMEs in EC Research and Development Programmes

### COM(87) 444/2/Revision final: Framework programme for Community activities in the field of research and technological development 1987-1991

This programme spells out the aims of Community research and development policy and the conditions for participation in the various programmes. The last inventory of the specific programmes was published by DG XII (Science, Research and Development), updating to 16 January 1989. The conditions for participation constitute in practice a hindrance to SMEs, and an effort has been made over the last two years to address the problems of:

Small and Medium Sized Enterprises

1. Information.   European Business Information Centres
   (EBICs) have a role here, with a new training
   programme for them in 1989 on R & D programmes and
   sources of finance.

2. Transnational collaboration.  Programmes like EUREKA
   are interested in future use of the BC-NET to help
   SMEs find suitable cross-national partners.   SMEs
   should note that BC-NET will in effect be developing
   a specialized R & D co-operation network.

3. The high cost of applying and the long time delays.
   As we shall see below, DG XII has developed a new
   scheme of feasibility awards for SMEs under the
   BRITE/EURAM programme, with the hope that this
   approach can be later applied to other programmes.

The Commission's Industrial Research and Development
Advisory Committee (IRDAC) set up a working party on
SMEs' contribution to the R & D process; the latter
concluded that their potential had not been realized and
that their problems needed to be addressed urgently.   In
particular, the competitiveness of many 'ordinary' SMEs
depended upon the application of the appropriate
technology in their production processes.   The rates of
SME direct participation in BRITE and ESPRIT have been
rising (around 20% in terms of full participants).
However, their role is less prominent in terms of the
budgetary value of the projects in which they are
involved and in terms of project leadership.   Most SMEs
take part indirectly through a large firm.
   Specific encouragement is being given to SMEs in two
senses:

1. The role of SMEs in less developed countries like
   Greece, Ireland and Portugal are being particularly
   promoted; and

2. Programme managers are to help as 'marriage brokers'
   for SMEs with other countries.   Accordingly, SMEs
   should directly approach programme managers for help
   in this way.

Small and Medium Sized Enterprises

SMEs should take note of these programmes if they are specialized and technology intensive and if they are prepared to be a part of consortia embracing large companies, universities and the public sector (e.g. research institutes). The industrially oriented programmes like BRITE/EURAM are especially relevant to them. They should also be aware that during 1988-9 the Commission was considering the idea of supporting SMEs from the stage of entering programmes through to the commercial stage of marketing.

COM(88) 385 Proposal for a Council decision on the BRITE/EURAM programme research and technological development programme in the fields of industrial manufacturing technologies and advanced materials (1989-1992)
This programme aims to support collaborative industrial research and technological development for the purpose of modernization of industrial sectors. It is a major programme, with an anticipated budget of 500 million ECUs and normally for bold, innovative projects of substantial size (total costs in the range 1-3 million ECUs and at least ten man-years of activity). It builds on two previously separate programmes: research in industrial technologies (BRITE) and advanced materials (EURAM).
SMEs with an interest in industrial applied research should note:

1. that contracts must be jointly funded by industry and the Commission;
2. that they must involve collaboration of at least two independent industrial enterprises, from different Member States;
3. that projects must fall within the technical areas of advanced materials technologies; design methodology and assurance for products and processes; application of manufacturing technologies; technologies for manufacturing processes; and research to develop the European aeronautical technology base; and
4. that applications can be made for feasibility awards

(more than 50 in 1989) for SMEs in order to help them demonstrate their abilities to potential partners in future collaborative proposals, particularly their role in the customer/supplier network.

Contact: DG XII, Directorate for Technological Research, rue de la Loi 200, B-1049 Brussels, tel: (02) 235 59 60 or 235 52 90.

ESPRIT II (European strategic programme for research and development in information technologies) December 1987-November 1992. Council Decision of 11 April 1988 Official Journal L118/1988.
RACE Programme (Research and development in advanced communications technologies in Europe) June 1987-May 1992. Council Decision of 14 December 1987. Official Journal L16/1988.
DELTA Programme (Development of European learning through technological advanced exploratory action) June 1988-May 1990. Council Decision of 29 June 1988. Official Journal L206/1988.
DRIVE Programme (Dedicated road infrastructure for vehicle safety in Europe) June 1988-May 1991. Council Decision of 29 June 1988. Official Journal L206/1988.
AIM Programme (Advanced informatics in medicine in Europe) 1988-1990 pilot phase. Council Decision of 4 November 1988. Official Journal L314/1988.
ECLAIR Programme (European collaborative linkage of agriculture and industry through research). COM(87) 667 proposal for a Council Decision.
FLAIR Programme (Food-linked agro-industrial research). COM(88) 351 final proposal for a Council Decision.
JOULE (Joint opportunities for unconventional or long-term energy supply) 1989-1992. COM(88) 388 final/2 Proposal for a Council Decision. Council Decision of 14 March 1989. Official Journal 89/236/EEC.
SMEs should be aware of these relevant R & D programmes in the fields of information and communication (ESPRIT II - 1600 million ECUs, RACE - 550 million ECUs, DELTA - 20 million ECUs, DRIVE - 60 million ECUs and AIM - 20 million ECUs), of biological

Small and Medium Sized Enterprises

resources (ECLAIR - 80 million ECUs and FLAIR - 25 million ECUs) and of non-nuclear energy programmes (JOULE - 122 million ECUs), including the hydrocarbons sector. They should also note the 'marriage-broker' function of programme managers and contact: for ESPRIT II-DG XII tel: (02) 236 20 67; RACE-DG XIII tel: (02) 235 92 35; DELTA-DG XIII tel: (02) 235 02 89; DRIVE-DG XIII tel: (02) 236 24 76; AIM-DG XIII tel: (02) 235 53 83; ECLAIR-DG XII tel: (02) 236 31 64; FLAIR-DG XII tel: (02) 236 31 64; and JOULE-DG XIII tel: (02) 235 39 78.


## Promoting SMEs in Innovation Policies

SPRINT Programme (Strategic programme for innovation and technology transfer). Council Decision 83/624/EC concerning a plan for transnational development of the supporting infrastructure for innovation and technology transfer. Council Decision (Official Journal L153 13 June 1987) on the 'SPRINT' programme.
COM(88) 747 final: Fourth annual report (1987) on SPRINT
The SPRINT programme aims to promote transnational technology transfer and assist industrial innovation and dynamism, particularly amongst SMEs, by granting EC support to organizations acting as intermediaries in the enterprise sector and participating in transnational cooperative groupings and by measures to diffuse new technologies and support industrial design. On 6 March 1989 the Council of Ministers allocated 90 million ECUs for the SPRINT programme 1989-93. SPRINT is the continuation, under a new name, of the 'transnational innovation plan' of 1983 and involves DG XIII in collaboration with the Business Co-operation Centre (BCC) and the European Association for the Transfer of Innovation Technologies and Industrial Information (T11). Encouragement of all aspects of the innovation process - from invention through to financing and marketing of new products and services - is pursued by the following activities.

1. The promotion of transnational co-operation between

technology and innovation management advisory bodies, linking up public and private business consultancy organizations (e.g. regional development agencies, chambers of commerce, technology and licence brokers, industrial liaison offices of universities), with the specific task of promoting transnational technological co-operation particularly between SMEs. By January 1989 some fifty technology transfer micro-networks had been established, involving about 170 SPRINT contractors; they had enabled EC support to be given to more than 120 transnational technological co-operation agreements, mostly amongst SMEs in different Member States, and in fields as varied as robotics and road traffic management. The networks covered the areas of innovation management (working with T11), full utilization of university research, applied research between technical industrial centres, design and finance (by forming the European Venture Capital Association, EVCA).

2. The promotion of transnational co-operation between industrial research associations, technical institutes and other similar bodies, the aim being to foster technology transfer towards, and innovation in specific sectors. By January 1989 SPRINT was supporting sixteen such projects between ninety-four industrial research associations in the EC e.g. to improve quality control in SMEs which process composite materials, the use of CAD/CAM by SMEs in the footwear sector, the adoption of laser-based material processing technology by SMEs, the adoption of quality management systems by SMEs in welding fabrication, the use of new technology by SMEs in the food sector.

3. These networks and agreements form the basis for further supportive action to aid technology transfer and innovation, notably European conferences and workshops on technology and innovation, organizing tours of technology trade fairs, circulating articles on public research systematically in the specialist press (especially through the co-operative network

Euro Tech Alert), transnational exchanges of professional personnel (a special scheme) and the setting up of the Comparative Index of National Standards in Europe (ICONE) which renders more transparent the national systems of technical standards and regulation.

4. Concertation between Member States and the EC on measures designed to promote technology transfer and innovation in such areas as fiscal policy, design, industrial patents rights and modernization of traditional sectors (ceramics, textiles, footwear).

5. Establishment of liaison mechanisms between local authorities in order to foster innovation.

6. Training of technology transfer specialists in the management and financing of innovation in firms.

7. A special scheme aims to promote design awareness.

Contact: DG XIII/C/2 (Telecommunications, Information Industries and Innovation), L-2920 Luxembourg, tel: (Lux) 4301 4180, and read its newsletter 'Innovation and Technology Transfer' for details of SPRINT - sponsored advisory bodies and their partners. SMEs should contact these advisory bodies directly if they think that their innovations, new products and processes are eligible for applications abroad.

T11 is concerned with the standards, status and professional development of organizations involved in technology transfer and aims to provide information and services to its members and promote transnational collaboration in the profession. Note in particular its newsletter 'T11 Focus' and its news leaflet 'T11 News'. T11 has over 250 members, and its activities are integrated into the SPRINT programme from which it receives a subsidy. Contact: T11, 3 rue des Capucins, L-1313 Luxembourg, tel: (Lux) 46 21 85.

**European Business and Innovatory Centres 1988, European**

Small and Medium Sized Enterprises

Business and Innovation Centre Network (EBN), Brussels, February 1989.
Model for Business and Innovation Centres, DG XVI, 1984.
EBN, Manual of Best Practices, Brussels, 1985.
The concept of BICs (Business and Innovation Centres) was born out of the thinking behind the ERDF Regulation of 1984 (1787/84) on mobilizing the indigenous development potential of 'less-favoured' regions by emphasizing SMEs and 'state-of-the-art' technology. DG XVI was concerned that most existing SME promotion agencies were not sufficiently selective in focusing their efforts on innovative, technology-based business 'start-ups' that were likely to have a significant long-term impact on local economic development. A BIC involved the notion of a 'hands-on' approach to launching 'start-up' companies, providing 'intensive care' in order to accelerate the development of carefully selected companies. Its purpose was to generate innovative, mostly technology-based 'start-ups' and to reduce their failure rate and increase their growth rate by the provision of a comprehensive range of facilities and advisory services. A BIC would become the focal point of a broadly-based federation of local interests, including SME promotion agencies, private companies, banks, educational establishments and public authorities. It was also to operate as a business in its own right and become self-financing. A BIC was to combine twelve functions: promotion/PR; detection of candidate entrepreneurs; evaluation and selection; entrepreneur training; business planning; marketing assistance; technology transfer; finance; professional services; 'incubator' space; logistical services; and business development.

In essence, the BIC concept had different sources: the shift of regional policy thinking from infrastructural provision and 'growth poles' to indigenous development potential; American experience with science parks and business incubator centres and university 'spin-offs' in high technology and with the role of SMEs in employment creation; and the desire to harness a proliferating number of enterprise support agencies (science parks, enterprise agencies etc) to EC

policy objectives.   In order to ensure that local development efforts were effectively linked into international networks and to promote and safeguard the BIC concept of public-private partnership, the European Business and Innovation Centre Network (EBN) was founded in 1984/5.   EBN's action programme involved setting up communication links between BICs; establishing a data base linking all BICs and containing details of their client SMEs; training of BIC managers to operate Centres and support SMEs; organization of conferences, seminars, regional twinnings and brokerage meetings; and identifying sources of finance.   ERDF support may be given to local promoters of BICs in one of the designated 'promotion zones'.
The first major EBN study (1989) is likely to prove a landmark in its development.   It reveals in particular the following characteristics of BICs.

1. In June 1987 the EBN network had thirty-eight full members, of which eighteen could be considered operational; of the operational BICs most were concentrated in West Germany (5), Britain (4), France (3) and the Netherlands (3); sixteen were close to a university and ten were urban-centred; capital investment appeared to be relatively high (compared to the US), with more dependence on public subsidy; the average number of staff was six to seven, with a bias towards business development and marketing and financial advice rather than technology advisory and training services; eleven were purpose-built units; and occupancy rates averaged 87% (ranging from 25% to 100%).

2. BICs tend to support a larger number of smaller tenant companies than science parks, technology centres and business incubators.   However, none of the BICs had attained the objective of creating at least ten new innovative businesses per year (the average was four to five), and only four were successfully managed as 'businesses in their own right'.   The largest BICs in terms of tenant company employees were Warwick (UK) with 600; Birmingham (UK)

with 550; Dortmund (West Germany) with 450; Limerick (Ireland) with 449; and Berlin with 400.

3. The key conditions for success for a BIC were: first-class real estate; good connection to a university or research establishment; seed capital provision; a mixture of knowledge-based firms, including some 'start-ups'; and defining a niche as a centre of excellence in one or two technological areas.

This report unleashed a conflict between DG XVI and the EBN management about the future direction of development and about the need for greater clarity about the BIC concept. DG XVI was more interested in the regional role of BICs as focal points for development and took a public-sector view of them; the EBN had a more commercial and private-sector orientation and wanted to move away from public subsidy. DG XVI was concerned to remove the existing EBN management and to introduce a new executive board to be elected by the BICs themselves and perhaps coming out of their own staff; the EBN wanted to maintain its existing autonomy of operation. DG XVI was also keen to strengthen the training of BIC managers.

Contact: EBN, rue Froissart 89, Box 5, B-1040 Brussels, tel: (02) 231 07 47.

COM(86) 723 Communication from the Commission to the Council and the European Parliament: Financial engineering

This proposal seeks to develop a Community policy of financial engineering which aims to satisfy funding needs that are not satisfactorily met by the market and to promote risk capital and secondary capital markets for SMEs consistent with the SME Action Programme. New initiatives in financial engineering are to help SMEs by:

1. increasing the supply of funds lent to finance SMEs' capital investment (see NCI IV and V, EIB and ECSC loans);

2. enabling access to credit for firms whose financial standing is too low to provide adequate security (development of mutual guarantee machinery);
3. increasing the equity capital of SMEs though the Venture Consort scheme and promotion of the EVCA;
4. providing funds for innovation (see SPRINT); and
5. using the Integrated Development Operations (IDOs) and Integrated Mediterranean Programmes (IMPs) to undertake experimental actions such as the establishment of regional venture capital operations and mutual guarantee funds.

In these ways the EC hoped to meet the key problems facing SMEs in being over-dependent on (short-term) loan finance compared to equity capital, in having higher interest rate costs than larger companies and in funding start-up capital.

Of particular interest to SMEs is the <u>Venture Consort</u> pilot scheme, jointly organized since 1985 by the EVCA and DG XIII. It aims to encourage the growth of European SMEs through the formation of cross-border syndicates of venture capitalists to finance cross-border innovative projects and drawing on risk capital from different countries. The establishment of EVCA in 1983 was also supported under the SPRINT programme. EVCA has about 180 active and supporting members from twenty-three countries and aims to promote and co-ordinate the development of the venture capital profession at the European level. In practice, only a minor number of venture capital investments have been made on a cross-border basis. EC Commission perceptions of its role in venture capital have changed, with the emphasis now being placed on the need for action at the national rather than EC level. The Venture Consort scheme is small, undersubscribed and unlikely to develop. In order to meet this problem EVCA has established a Business Development Committee which will be on the look-out for companies that, with the right type of backing, could become pan-European success stories. The approach of the EC Commission is likely to remain small-scale and indirect, focusing on creating networks amongst venture capitalists and in the secondary securities market and on stimulating the investment capacity of venture capital organizations. Under a pilot project, <u>Eurotech Capital</u>, beginning in 1989, the EC will grant financial aid to venture capital organizations which will on-lend the funds for the development of transnational high technology projects, with priority to SMEs. Contact: EVCA, 11F clos du Parnasse, B-1040 Brussels, tel: (02) 513 74 39.

The Commission and the European Investment Bank have also supported the creation of the European Financial Engineering Company (EFEC). This public-limited company groups together the majority of institutions which specialize in long-term credit and the acquisition of holdings in different EC countries. EFEC puts special emphasis on supporting the national and transnational innovation plans of SMEs by offering a complete range of financial engineering services. Contact: EFEC, 10 boulevard Royal, L-2449 Luxembourg, tel: (Lux) 46 07 10.

## EC Commission, A Community pilot action to stimulate seed capital, preliminary document, 1989

This proposed five-year pilot scheme recognizes that the venture capital field is much more professionally developed in the EC than the provision of seed capital and that consequently there is a serious gap in support for innovation by SMEs. In particular, the experience of the BICs (see p106) in their first years of operation has clearly pointed to the lack of seed capital as an important constraint on their effectiveness. According to EVCA, only 4% of new investments undertaken by venture capitalists in 1986 was directed towards seed capital.

The provision of seed capital involves investment in new or embryonic companies, making available to them resources to develop a product prototype and a business strategy to a point where a commercial decision on venture capital or more traditional forms of finance can be considered. In other words, it is concerned with backing projects that are in the process of being transformed into an enterprise.

The draft proposal seeks to create an EC-wide network

of up to twenty-four seed capital funds, with an important number of them to be in assisted areas covered by the ERDF, IMPs and the ECSC. Generally, funds would be eligible for an interest-free advance; in assisted areas they would also receive a capital contribution, preferably channelled through the local BIC which will have an important monitoring role. In this way the role of BICs could be strengthened. The new network would exchange information, experience and expertise amongst the funds and develop a training scheme for seed capital fund managers. It would also have close links to other networks like EBN, BC-NET and EVCA. The seed capital funds would acquire equity holdings in new or embryonic companies.

This proposal could be one of the most important for European SMEs in helping to fund innovative projects through the critical early stages of development. Particularly for high-tech schemes, venture capital companies and banks often view very early funding as too risky or too long-term. The EC plans to raise up to 1,000 million ECUs every year until 1994 to give seed funds for SMEs. However, the proposal could run into opposition from Britain, the Netherlands and West Germany. The problem is that the EC Commission wants to raise the funds on the capital markets and has proposed a mechanism that would allow it to recycle the loans. Some Member States do not want the Commission to act like a bank.

A call for expressions of interest in participating in a pilot action has been published (Official Journal 1 December 1988). Contact: DG XXIII, tel: (02) 235 62 69.


**Promoting SMEs by Loan Finance Support**

EIB-Information, European Investment Bank, February 1989, No 59, European Investment Bank annual report 1987, European Investment Bank, 1988.
COM(88) 244 final Communication from the Commission: The EIB, the other financial instruments and strengthening economic and social cohesion.

COM(88) 692 final: Commission report to the Council and to the Parliament on the borrowing and lending activities of the Community in 1987.
Council Decision No 78/870 16 October 1978 setting up the New Community Instrument (NCI).
COM(88) 661 final: Proposal for a Council Decision on NCI V.

The European Investment Bank (EIB) was established under Article 129 of the Treaty of Rome as the EC's major investment finance body, independent of the other EC institutions. It on-lends, at near to its cost of borrowing on capital markets, to firms, financial institutions and public authorities for capital investments meeting specific EC priorities (the development of 'less-favoured' regions, the modernization or conversion of sectors, or projects in the 'common interest' of the EC). The EIB offers two types of loan: (1) individual loans to larger industrial projects and (2) global loans, via an intermediary financial institution, to provide a credit line, for a fixed amount, for on-lending to finance smaller-scale investments that conform with the EIB's lending criteria. Global loans cover projects in the productive sector, advanced technology projects and energy-saving projects.

The New Community Instrument (NCI) was created in October 1978, with the aim of increasing the combined credit capacity of the EC and of providing another finance source for investment projects furthering economic objectives to which the EC attaches particular priority. NCI II (April 1982) and NCI III (April 1983) made SMEs a priority (alongside regional development and energy); NCI IV (November 1986) made SMEs the priority, with particular stress on very small firms, and the EIB was requested to provide the same scale of loan facility from its own resources for the same purpose; whilst the proposed NCI V (1989) restated the exclusive focus on SMEs and emphasized the two areas of advanced technology and diversification of the rural economy.

Whereas the EIB is first and foremost dedicated to banking criteria, the NCI reflects the EC's political priorities more clearly and is thus controversial. In fact, opposition has grown with each new authorization, particularly from Britain, the Netherlands and West Germany. At the same time the NCI has been influential as a lever on the EIB and as an indicator to the financial markets in general. This emulative effect was apparent under NCI IV when the EIB accepted the 'request' to match the NCI support for SMEs.

In 1988 loans from the EIB (inside and outside the EC) totalled over 10 billion ECUs for the first time. Of the total of 9,474.8 million ECUs inside the EC, 365.5 billion came from the resources of the NCI. There was a notably brisk growth of credit for SMEs, with over 5,200 of them receiving funds under global loans. Of the total of 2.9 billion ECUs of financing for the productive sector, 1.8 billion ECUs (a marked increase) went to SMEs under global loans. The bulk of the global loans were for SME investment projects in the 'less-favoured' areas, notably Portugal, Greece, Ireland, Spain and Italy. Under NCI IV a total of thirty-two global loans were granted to nineteen intermediary institutions in six EC states in 1987. The cumulative total of NCI global loans granted for the modernization of SMEs was 924 sub-loans totalling 285 million ECUs, with Italy (44%), Spain (25%) and France (17%) being the main recipients.

From the European Year of the SME in 1983 to 1988, the EIB has contributed from its own and NCI resources to the financing of a total of some 25,000 productive investment schemes of SMEs, for a total of some 7.7 billion ECUs. This total involves almost 14,500 SMEs (4.3 billion ECUs) from EIB resources and 9,820 SMEs (2.7 billion ECUs) from NCI resources.

Contact: EIB Head Office, 100 boulevard Konrad Adenauer, L-2950 Luxembourg tel: (Lux) 4379-1, and the EIB office in the relevant Member State. For NCI, contact: DG II (Economic and Financial Affairs), 200 rue de la Loi, B-1049 Brussels, tel: (02) 235 15 58 or 235 56 77.

SMEs should also note that European Coal and Steel Community (ECSC) loans can be attractive to prospective investors located in ECSC regions adversely affected by the decline of coal and steel activities. Generous investment rebates are available for certain projects creating long-term employment opportunities for redundant ECSC workers under Article 56 of the Paris Treaty (18 April 1951). Particularly relevant for SMEs are: (1) Article 56(2)(a) 'soft' reconversion loans which have been increasingly directed at providing seed capital to SMEs; and (2) Article 56(2)(b) readaption aid which has evolved towards 'active' aid for self-employment. These loans may be granted directly to the promoter or through the global loan system. SMEs should contact for direct loan applications under Article 56 either DG XVI (Regional Policy) tel: (02) 235 8468 or DG V (Employment, Social Affairs and Education) tel: (02) 235 1550; and for global loans the list of national financial intermediaries most frequently used. Loans granted under Article 56 increased by 24% in 1987.


## Promoting Business Co-operation Amongst SMEs

COM(87) 370 final Communication from the Commission, Business Co-operation Network (BC-NET), strengthening of co-operation between European firms.
COM(88) 162 final Communication from the Commission, strengthening co-operation between European firms: A response to the 1992 internal market deadline.
   The Business Co-operation Centre (BCC), nicknamed the 'Marriage Bureau', was established in 1973, became an integral part of the SME Task-Force in 1986 and, in 1989, was subsumed under DG XXIII. A renewed emphasis on strengthening support for co-operation between SMEs was notably apparent in the SME Action Programme of 1986 and in the SPRINT programme on technological co-operation as well as in research and development e.g. BRITE/EURAM (see p102). Co-operation was important not just in securing greater cohesion amongst the EC Member States but, above all, in ensuring that SMEs were given every opportunity to expand and innovate within the Single European Market. SMEs must be enabled to work together, without losing their own individuality, in order to help each other to increase their competitiveness, efficiency and market penetration. Co-

operation could help SMEs to gain access to new technologies, expand product ranges, minimize market costs, achieve economies of scale in production and marketing, guarantee security of supplies, and limit the need to set up in another country. Various forms of co-operation are possible: technical, financial or commercial. Also, co-operation may be contractual (e.g. through a European Economic Interest Grouping) or informal and involve two partners or a whole network.

The BCC aims to provide an infrastructure of support to help SMEs overcome the extra problems and costs that they face in launching into interregional or cross-frontier operations. It will assist SMEs to find partners to cooperate in one or more of four areas:

1. technical e.g. R & D, technology, exchange of know how, patents, licenses, manufacturing arrangements;
2. commercial e.g. marketing, distribution, supply of equipment, commercial agreements;
3. financial e.g. business creation, takeovers, mergers, joint ventures, reciprocal participations; and
4. subcontracting (see later).

In pursuit of this mission of encouraging co-operation amongst SMEs the BCC has four main tasks (two others are dealt with in separate sections directly below).

1. The traditional task of BCC is to process and disseminate requests for, and offers of co-operation sent in directly by, SMEs. SMEs are asked to fill in questionnaires which are sent to business consultants in the Member States; the latter ensure publicity through their own bulletins and data banks.

2. BC-NET (the Business Co-operation Network) is a more sophisticated co-operation tool. This computerized system has been operational since July 1988 for an experimental period of two years and links up business advisers across the EC (e.g. private consultants, chambers of commerce, banks, enterprise or development agencies, solicitors) in order to

expedite the process of matching companies. The SME Task-Force selected 350 business advisers from all Member States and intends to develop its network outside the EC. During the first four months the BC-NET received some 3,700 'co-operation profiles', suggesting a flow of around 15,000 CPs per year. The matching rate was about 10% and was expected to reach 15% when new telecommunications facilities make the 'flash profile' possible. In July 1989 approximately 150 advisers should be able to use the BC-NET system from their offices by using PCs. This number was expected to double by the beginning of 1990.

SMEs should note how BC-NET works. A SME should first approach one of the business advisers who will introduce the company's request for co-operation into the system using a common language called a 'co-operation profile'. The BC-NET system automatically compares the request with its stock of offers. If a positive match is found, the requesting company and the companies offering co-operation are immediately informed. If the response is negative, the profile can be automatically distributed as a 'flash profile' to those BC-NET advisers in the geographical area covered by the request. This latter facility is optional. In order to ensure confidentiality the relevant business advisers will get into contact with each other; SMEs do not have direct access to BC-NET. Also, whilst the agreement between the EC and the members of BC-NET forbids advisers to make a profit out of this operation, they may charge for the service. It is likely that after 1990 the EC Commission will entrust the management of BC-NET to the advisers.

3. BCC helps to implement different EC policies that seek to promote co-operation. It seeks in particular to encourage greater SME participation in the EC's R & D programme (see above) and in innovation and technology transfer through the SPRINT programme (see above).

4. BCC attempts to extend co-operation to those non-EC

states with which agreements exist, notably Australia, Austria, Brazil, Canada, Finland, India, Tunisia, Sweden, Switzerland and Yugoslavia.

Contact:  Business Co-operation Centre, DG XXIII, 80 rue d'Arlon, B-1040 Brussels, tel: (02) 235 55 68 or 235 60 12 (for BC-NET).

COM(88) 162 final Communication from the Commission, ibid.  Catalogue Europartenariat 89, available from DG XXIII.

This Commission document identifies 'Europartnership' as one of two current developments in the field of building a European network of business co-operation. 'Europartnership' seeks to exploit the indigenous potential in regions which are lagging in development or suffering industrial decline, by promoting co-operation agreements between firms of a particular region and firms in other regions of the EC.  The scheme brings together ideas of the SME Action Programme and DG XVI's stress on SMEs as motors of internally generated development.  Private-sector resources are to be mobilized to dovetail with governments' regional development initiatives.  'Europartnership' is distinctive from traditional support for co-operation amongst SMEs in its 'activist' approach to generating a significant volume of co-operation agreements, which it will monitor and follow up, in all sectors of production.  It is envisaged as a catalyst on behalf of SPRINT, COMETT, ERDF and ESF.

This joint initiative of the SME Task-Force and DG XVI began with a pilot project, 'Europartnership 88', in Ireland.  The pilot project had three stages: (1) a market research stage, in which the characteristics of the local industrial structure, the needs, the potential for co-operation and the likely sectors were identified; (2) production of a catalogue, covering suitable projects for co-operation, for dissemination in other EC states through the correspondents of the BCC, BICs and other suitable bodies; and (3) organization of a meeting (in Dublin) to put local businesses with co-operation plans in touch with businesses from other EC states. 'Europartnership 88' was evaluated as a success (with some 800 visitors and 117 Irish firms and 186 firms from the other EC states involved, leading to more than 500 contacts); a survey of participating Irish companies (response rate of 55%) discovered that 6% reacted 'very positively' about established contacts, 46% 'positively', 36% 'negatively' and 12% 'very negatively'. It was felt that the catalogue should be available earlier, at least five months before the meeting. 'Europartnership 89' was planned for June 1989, with Andalusia as the chosen site; out of a total of 703 interested companies 221 were chosen for the catalogue.

In the context of promoting transnational co-operation amongst SMEs in 'less-favoured' regions two other initiatives are relevant: (1) a practical guide for SMEs on steps to take to find a partner, to be published in 1989; and (2) the joint project on regional co-operation to assist SMEs to find partners between the BICs of Bordeaux, Barcelona, Milan and Lyon.

Contact: BCC (as above).


COM(88) 162 final. Communication from the Commission, ibid.
Sub-contracting in Europe Conference, May 1988, final report, SME Task-Force, pp194, 1988.

This Commission document identifies the promotion of trans-national sub-contracting as the second main development in building a European network of business co-operation. Commission policy has the following main dimensions:

1. Greater understanding by an analysis (technical, economic and legal) of the phenomenon of sub-contracting, particularly in Europe, from both the macro-economic and sectoral perspectives. An analysis of economic flows in transnational sub-contracting in Europe was being prepared for the end of 1988. Sub-contracting relationships, in which a company works for another company with a view to

design or manufacture of a specific product, are seen as evolving in quantity and complexity (with the acceleration of technical progress and under the impetus of greater international competition) and as requiring a new relationship or partnership, based on more stable relations between a main contractor and a limited number of companies. Only in this way can the Japanese 'just-in-time' production system be applied to accelerate materials flow and thus reduce stock levels. The EC is seen as a long way behind Japan in its approach to the organization of production. Large companies must be encouraged to exploit the advantages of sub-contracting (e.g. by helping with equipment or initial investment), whilst sub-contractors have to rely increasingly on computer integrated manufacturing.

2. Improvement of relations between main contractors and sub-contractors. Better communications were pursued in three ways:

1) In the early 1980s an initiative was launched to provide multilingual sectoral terminologies, to be mainly used on an international scale for establishing data banks and for the administration of sub-contracting grants. Two are already available - metal, and plastics and rubber; four are being prepared - electronics and the electrical industry, industrial services, textiles, and wood and its by-products.

2) Publication of a sub-contracting vade-mecum, a practical guide to sub-contractors on the legal aspects of sub-contracts in the EC, to enable them to enter into fair and balanced transnational agreements more easily.

3) BC-NET is seen as an important tool in promoting sub-contracting on a European level, whilst consideration is also being given to the possibility of creating a European centre for sub-contracting to bring together existing documentation, to provide a forum for study and contacts, and to assist sub-contractors wishing to

tender for public procurement contracts in other EC countries. At present the BCC remains the major contact.

3. Support for the modernization efforts of sub-contracting SMEs. The Commission has launched a pilot training scheme for managers and employees of SMEs in 'just-in-time' techniques. A more extensive scheme is planned in this field. Consideration is being given to quality control and certification, with a view to the possibility of an EC initiative. Mutual recognition of certification procedures and test results is essential in order to reduce sub-contracting problems.

Transnational sub-contracting is scheduled as a major growth area for EC action. Contact: the BCC (as above).


The European economic interest grouping (EEIG).
   See p.78.


**Providing Information for SMEs**

COM(87) 152 final. Communication from the Commission, Centres for European business information.
COM(88) 161 final. Communication from the Commission, European information centres: Extension of the projects, evaluation of the European information centre project, 18 October 1988, SME Task-Force
COM(88) 693 final. Communication from the Commission, interim report on the extension of the European information centre project
   The European Information Centre (Euroguichet) project, established by the Commission in September 1987, was an integral part of the SME Action Programme and aimed to meet business requirements for up-to-date and comprehensive information about the EC, with particular reference to the Single European Market. These information requirements relate: (1) to EC programmes, services and contracts; and (2) to such

specific issues as tax law and company law in different EC states. They are also best met by a single intermediary which brings together the 'host' structure of traditional information and advisory services with EC documentation, data bases and information as well as specialist external data services. The 'host' structure may be local and regional bodies, banks or representative business or professional organizations, with experience in providing advice and assistance to businesses. The European Information Centre is to ensure a two-way and decentralized flow of information, acting as an information distribution network and as an interface between SMEs and the EC which can thereby gain a better understanding of SMEs' concerns. They are, accordingly, decentralized in operation.

The one-year pilot project involved thirty-nine European Information Centres. It was followed by an evaluation exercise, which judged the project to be a great success, and by the proposal to extend the project (by means of a 'call for tender') to promote both a comprehensive regional coverage of the EC and sectoral coverage through specialized European Information Centres (e.g. linked to trade associations). In all, up to 200 were envisaged, to be established progressively. 'Host' structures were chosen with particular reference to three criteria: representation of and/or proximity to SMEs, well-trained and knowledgeable staff, and financial capacity and willingness to invest in a non-profit making activity. They were expected to be able to improve the product through 'value-added' services e.g. courses, presence at trade fairs. In turn, the gains are considerable: regular up-dated EC documents, accessing external data bases, an electronic mail system covering the centres and creating a European information network, ongoing training of centre staff, and assistance of a central unit in dealing with questions.

The evaluation exercise revealed a rapid increase in utilization rate, with most questions relating to the Single European Market programme (24.2%), to research and development programmes (20.5%), to company law and public supply contracts (15.2%) and statistics (15.2%). Particularly promising were their roles as a transnational information network (e.g. tax and company law issues) and as correspondents of BC-NET in relaying information on transnational co-operation opportunities.

The next phase of European Information Centres envisages a diminishing Commission grant over subsequent years; thereafter the 'host' structure will have to support it. Though they are to remain non-profit making bodies, future financing policy has still (May 1989) to be resolved. The first thirty-nine pilot centres did not charge fees for use; the issue of future charging was left open. It is clear, however, that the centres will have to become self-financing, with the centre organizers providing the premises and staff.

In June 1989 the Commission announced that the present EC-wide network of thirty-nine European Information Centres was to be extended by opening a further 148 centres. At this rate of installation it is expected that the EC territory as a whole will be covered between July 1989 and mid-1990.

Developing a data base on European enterprises: Community statistical programme for 1989-1992.

This large programme aims to provide the EC with global and coherent statistical information and comparable data and includes a project for plotting the effect of the Single European Market on SMEs.

1. The Statistical Office of the EC is working with national statistical offices to provide data on the size distribution of enterprises by sector, with reference to employment and turnover.

2. Private consultants are being used to assess the quality of private-sector data bases, with the aim of conducting a statistical analysis to identify the average size of enterprises, by sector and by country.

Although the data base will incorporate large as well as small enterprises, it will enable the EC Commission to plot the impact of the Single European Market on the

## Small and Medium Sized Enterprises

size distribution of enterprises, by country and by sector, and will help SMEs to recognize themselves in relation to other enterprises. The aim is to publish a book on the condition of small businesses in the EC in 1990.

SECTION III
COMMISSION DOCUMENTS OF RELEVANCE TO SMALL AND MEDIUM
SIZED ENTERPRISES

# I: POLICY PROPOSALS AND MEMORANDA

- those not referred to in Section II.

COM(87) 388/2/Rev. final: Communication from the Commission to the Council on steel policy.

Council Decision of 5 October 1987 introducing a communications network Community Programme on trade electronic data interchange systems (TEDIS). Official Journal of the European Communities Legislation, 8 October 1987, 87/499/EEC.

COM(87) 275 final: Second communication from the Commission on shipbuilding - the industrial, social and regional impact.

COM(88) 134 final: Third report from the Commission to the Council and the European Parliament on the implementation of its White Paper on completing the internal market.

COM(87) 275/2/Rev. final: Revised version of the second communication from the Commission on shipbuilding.

COM(89) 38 final: Third report by the Community on the realization of the objectives of the Community action programme for SMEs.

Council Resolution of 30 June 1988 on the improvement of the business environment and action to promote the development of enterprises, especially SMEs, in the Community. Official Journal of the European Communities Information and Notices, 27 July 1988, 88/C197/04.

COM(88) 291 final: Communication from the Commission reinforcing co-operation between EUREKA and the EC.

Small and Medium Sized Enterprises

COM(88) 404 final: Communication from the Commission on the simplification of administrative procedures within the Community.

COM(89) 102 final:  Proposal for a Council Decision concerning the improvement of the business environment and action to promote the development of SMEs in the Community.

General Commission guidelines for the implementation of a specific industrial development programme (PEDIP) in 1988 and 1989.  Official Journal of the European Communities Information and Notices, 31 December 1988, 88/C336/05.

Guidelines concerning European Social Fund intervention in respect of action against long-term unemployment and occupational integration of young people.  Official Journal of the European Communities Information and Notices, 24 February 1989, 89/C43/04.

COM(88) 713 final:  Report of the Commission on the implementation of the resolution to combat unemployment amongst women.

COM(87) 355 final:  Recommendation for Council Decision on the conclusion of protocols and technical co-operation between the EEC and Tunisia, Egypt, Israel, Algeria and Jordan.

See Decision Nos    88/34/EEC        27 January 1988
                    88/33/EEC
                    88/32/EEC
                    88/31/EEC
                    88/30/EEC

COM(88) 136 - I & II:  Communication from the Commission: Relations between the Community and Japan.

COM(88) 241/2 final: Communication from the Commission: an enterprise policy for the Community, preparing the path for business in the single European market.

Small and Medium Sized Enterprises

Council Resolution of 5 June 1989 on continuing vocational training. Official Journal of the European Communities Information and Notices, 15 June 1989, 89/C148/01.

COM(89) 76 final: Europartnership: results and assessment.

COM(88) 244 final: Communication from the Commission: the European Investment Bank, the other financial instruments and strengthening economic and social cohesion.

Commission Decision of 4 May 1988 on the guidelines for the management of the European Social Fund in the financial years 1989 to 1991. Official Journal of the European Communities Legislation, 10 June 1988, 88/319/EEC.

COM(87) 521 final: Twelfth annual report from the Commission on the European Regional Development Fund.

COM(87) 360/2/Revision final: Communication from the Commission, together with a draft for a Council Decision, concerning establishment at Community level of a policy and a plan of priority actions for the development of an information services market.

COM(87) 319 final: Communication from the Commission on the Community support plan to facilitate access to large-scale scientific facilities of European interest (1988-92).

Own-initiative opinion of the Economic and Social Committee on 'A policy for upland areas'. Official Journal of the European Communities Information and Notices, 4 July 1988, 88/C175/16.

COM(88) 316 final: Amendment to the proposal for a Council recommendation to the Member States on developing the exploitation of renewable energy sources in the Community.

Small and Medium Sized Enterprises

COM(88) 114 final: Communication from the Commission on the promotion and financing of technological and industrial co-operation.

Guidelines for the examination of state aid in the fisheries sector. Official Journal of the European Communities Information and Notices, 8 December 1988, 88/C313/09.

COM(88) 413 final: Proposal for a Council Decision on an action programme for European Tourism Year (1990).

Proposal for a Council Decision establishing the LINGUA programme, to promote training in foreign languages in the EC. Official Journal of the European Communities Information and Notices, 28 February 1989, 89/C51/06.

## II.  COMMISSION INFORMATION PUBLICATIONS

Paolo Cecchini, The European Challenge 1992 - The Benefits of a Single Market, Wildwood House, Aldershot, 1988.

Club de Bruxelles, The future of SMEs in Europe. European News Agency, Brussels, 1988.

Club de Bruxelles, Towards a Single Market - How, why and when  European News Agency, Brussels, 1987.

Club de Bruxelles, What the EC can offer SMEs  European News Agency, Brussels, 1988.

Commission of the European Communities, Business in Europe: European Policy for SMEs, EC, Luxembourg, 1987.

Commission of the European Communities, Catalogue for the Europartenariat 89 meeting, EC, Luxembourg, 1989.

Commission of the European Communities, Guide for 1988 applicants on COMETT, EC, Luxembourg, 1987.

Commission of the European Communities, Social Europe: the social dimension of the internal market, EC, Luxembourg, 1988.

Commission of the European Communities Background

Small and Medium Sized Enterprises

Report, ISEC/B18/87, 24 September 1987. - the role of SMEs in the economy of the EC.


Commission of the European Communities Spokesman's Service Information Memo -

P.69, 8 June 1988    - Summary of proposals to amend the 4th and 7th Company Law Directives

P.130, 15 November 1988 - Summary of the Commission's proposal to adapt the New Community Instrument to new priority objectives.


Commission of the European Communities Spokesman's Service Press Release -

IP(88) 15, 13 January 1988 - UK government proposals to fund a new advisory scheme to promote better management and investment in SMEs.

IP(88) 60, 3 February 1988 - UK aid scheme to develop the marketing of SMEs in Northern Ireland.


EURO-INFO - newsletter produced by the SME Task-Force covering Community information of interest to SMEs.


European File:

3/88, February 1988 - Action programme for SMEs

11/88, June/July 1988 - EC and co-operation amongst SMEs.

12/88, June/July 1988 - European Financial Area


European Investment Bank - Information

Small and Medium Sized Enterprises

No 53. - Community support for SMEs - European Investment Bank and New Community Instrument IV.

European Investment Bank Press Release -

   RS 1/89 - Details of the EIB loan to Barclay's Bank for onlending to SMEs.

   RS 3/89 - Details of the EIB loan to the 3i Group to finance SMEs throughout the UK.

SME Task-Force, Practical Handbook on the Operations of SMEs in the European Community, (1988 edition), EC, Luxembourg 1988.

Target 1992 - monthly newsletter on the Single Internal Market.

## III. EUROPEAN PARLIAMENT AND ECONOMIC AND SOCIAL COMMITTEE DOCUMENTS

Report drawn up on behalf of the Committee on Regional Policy and Regional Planning on regional development, education and training.

European Parliament Working Documents, 10 November 1986, A 2-133/86.

Report drawn up on behalf of the Committee on Regional Policy and Regional Planning on the mountain regions.

European Communities European Parliament Reports, 27 May 1987, PE DOC A 2-82/87

Report drawn up on behalf of the Committee on Regional Policy and Regional Planning on one integrated development programme for Portugal

European Communities European Parliament Reports, 12 November 1987, PE DOC A 2-214/87

CES(87) 646: Opinion of the Economic and Social Committee on the action programmes for SMEs.

Report drawn up on behalf of the Committee on Economic and Monetary Affairs and Industrial Policy on the sixteenth report of the Commission on competition policy.

European Communities European Parliament Reports, 18 November 1987, PE DOC A 2-223/87

Small and Medium Sized Enterprises


COM(87) 732 final:  Report from the Commission to the
Council and the European Parliament:  Fifteenth Report
on the activities of the European Social Fund for the
financial year 1986.


Report drawn up on behalf of the Committee on Economic
and Monetary Affairs and Industrial Policy on the
proposal for a Directive supplementing the common system
of value added tax and amending Directive No 77/388/EEC:
Removal of fiscal frontiers.

   European Communities European Parliament Reports, 15
   December 1988, PE DOC A 2-320/88